DEALING WITH A NARCISSIST

Understanding and Engaging the Narcissist in Your Life

PRISCILLA POSEY

© **Copyright 2019 by Priscilla Posey - All rights reserved.**

This book is provided with the sole purpose of providing relevant information on a specific topic for which every reasonable effort has been made to ensure that it is both accurate and reasonable. Nevertheless, by purchasing this book, you consent to the fact that the author, as well as the publisher, are in no way experts on the topics contained herein, regardless of any claims as such that may be made within. As such, any suggestions or recommendations that are made within are done so purely for entertainment value. It is recommended that you always consult a professional prior to undertaking any of the advice or techniques discussed within.

This is a legally binding declaration that is considered both valid and fair by both the Committee of Publishers Association and the American Bar Association and should be considered as legally binding within the United States.

The reproduction, transmission, and duplication of any of the content found herein, including any specific or extended information will be done as an illegal act regardless of the end form the information ultimately takes. This includes copied versions of the work both physical, digital, and audio unless express consent of the Publisher is provided beforehand. Any additional rights reserved.

Furthermore, the information that can be found within the pages described forthwith shall be considered both accurate and truthful when it comes to the recounting of facts. As such, any use, correct or incorrect, of the provided information will render the Publisher free of responsibility as to the actions taken outside of their direct purview. Regardless, there are zero scenarios where the original author or the Publisher can be deemed liable in any fashion for any damages or hardships that may result from any of the information discussed herein.

Additionally, the information in the following pages is intended only for informational purposes and should thus be thought of as universal. As befitting its nature, it is presented without assurance regarding its prolonged validity or interim quality. Trademarks that are mentioned are done without written consent and can in no way be considered an endorsement from the trademark holder.

Table of Contents

Introduction..v

Section 1: The Narcissistic Mind

Chapter 1: Narcissistic Personality Disorder 3

Chapter 2: Everyday Narcissism 14

Chapter 3: Secret Feelings.. 26

Chapter 4: The Perfectionism Problem................... 35

Section 2: Engaging the Narcissist

Chapter 5: Therapeutic Approaches 47

Chapter 6: Assessment & Identification.................. 60

Chapter 7: The Narcissist's Awareness 77

Chapter 8: Maintaining Yourself 84

Chapter 9: Different Contexts 94

Section 3: Working with Others outside the Circle

Chapter 10: Family and Triggers 109

Chapter 11: Best Friends & Platonic Loves 116

Chapter 12: Kids Involved....................................... 122

Section 4: Bonus Chapters

Chapter 13: Helpful Mobile Apps to Make Dealing with a Narcissist Bearable........................ 135

Chapter 14: 25 Helpful Affirmations for Dealing with a Narcissist 142

Conclusion... 163

References, Resources, and Helpful Links.............. 167

INTRODUCTION

I was just 19 when I had my first encounter with a narcissist. He was charming and handsome, and his smile alone could light up the entire room. When we locked eyes, it was like we had an instant connection. Despite meeting at a party in college, we spent the entire night outside, just talking with one another. We had similar hobbies, enjoyed the same movies, and we even both shared a love for the taco stand just off campus that most people never bothered giving the time of day.

I told him all about how I had deliberately chosen a college far away from home to escape from my parents who were far too overbearing for my taste, discussed my hopes and dreams for the future, and he told me a bit about himself as well. We immediately kicked off what I thought would be a lifelong friendship. Within two weeks, we were exclusively dating. After four months, he proposed and I said yes and moved in with him. One year later, we were married, and just two months later, I was pregnant with my daughter at the young age of 20.

Once the rings were on our fingers, his personality shifted completely, something I now understand as him finding the persona he used to attract me was no longer necessary. My husband, who I loved deeply, began to grow distant. He would criticize everything. Nothing I did was as good as him. If I scored less than 100% in a class, he would tell me I wasn't smart enough to be going to college, and it was a waste of money to keep paying for my tuition when I would be a stay at home parent anyway, something he decided with no input from me. If dinner wasn't perfect, he would throw it all in the garbage and order a pizza, but if he burnt something, I was not allowed to say a word about it without enraging him. If his clothes were not perfectly ironed for work when he got up in the morning, he would wake me up and insist I do it for him because it was my job, even if that woke our daughter in the process. If I tried to protest at all, he would remind me that my job was to maintain our home, care for our daughter, and get perfect scores in the class. Anything less than that was absolutely unacceptable.

I was convinced I had to do what he asked. After all, he went to work for us, so his expectations weren't unreasonable. Of course, it would fall on me to take care of the home and our daughter. And it made sense that I had to score as highly as possible because I wanted the best bang for my tuition. He only wanted what was best for me because he loved me, so he held me to a higher standard than other people. That made sense to me.

Over time, his criticisms of me became more direct. He would call me fat if I ate something he didn't approve of, or tell me to change my clothes or makeup if he thought my shirt was too low-cut or my makeup was too provocative. If I protested, he accused me of cheating. Eventually, it got to the point where I felt like I could do nothing without running it by him first and confirming everything was to his impossible standards, and even that was not good enough. I couldn't do it anymore, and once I came to that revelation, I suddenly felt a little freer.

When I finally began to open up to others, one of my friends suggested I look into narcissism. Imagine my surprise as I read through the criteria for being diagnosed with narcissistic personality disorder and discovering that my husband met most of them. That began the start of a new journey, and I began delving into any material I could find on the subject. The more I read, the more it all made sense. Then began my journey of disentangling myself from my ex. I had to escape his grasp one claw at a time to disengage from the relationship, and I have never been happier now that I am free. My narcissistic ex was downright toxic, but yours may not be. You may be able to salvage your relationship with some of the techniques provided in this book if you think it is worthwhile.

I eventually managed to more or less recover from my period with my narcissistic ex, and now it is time to pass on my wisdom to those trying to escape or heal from their own narcissistic abuse. This book is my comprehensive guide to what narcissistic minds are, how to best engage a narcissist, how to interact with others in regards to supporting you in your journey, and some bonus chapters that I found might provide some useful content. Hopefully, you will find this book useful as you begin your journey to understanding the narcissistic mind, and you will find valuable insight into why narcissists do what they do.

As A Token of My Gratitude...

I'd like to offer you this amazing resource which my clients pay for. It is a report I written when I first began my journey.

Click on the picture above or navigate to the website below to join my exclusive email list. Upon joining, you will receive this incredible report on how to recognize an abusive relationship.

If you ask most people on the street what an abusive relationship is, chances are you'd get a description of physical abuse. And yes, that is most certainly an abusive relationship. However, abuse comes in many forms. The actual meaning of abuse is when someone exerts control over another person.

Find out more about recognizing an abusive relationship and learn how to take control over your life by clicking on the book above or by going to this link:

http://bit.ly/RecognizeAbusiveRelationship

SECTION 1
The Narcissistic Mind

Dealing with a Narcissist

CHAPTER 1

Narcissistic Personality Disorder

Narcissistic personality disorder: It sounds as intimidating as it is. This disorder is primarily characterized by grandiose or self-important behavior, a constant desire for attention, and a lack of empathy. This is behavior that is common and expected in children, but narcissists are adults that never outgrew this childish way of thinking. However, being diagnosed with narcissistic personality disorder (NPD) requires more than a childish way of thinking. The fifth edition of the Diagnostic and Statistical Manual of Mental Disorders (DSM-5) has identified nine specific behavioral patterns or traits that are relevant to NPD. If a person has at least five of the nine specified behaviors in a wide range of situations or circumstances, they qualify for a diagnosis. People with less than five are not diagnosed with NPD, but the narcissistic tendencies can still be particularly toxic or harmful for those the person targets.

A grandiose sense of self-importance

Perhaps one of the most recognizable traits of those with NPD is the grandiosity or superiority complexes narcissists possess. The narcissist believes that he is the most important person in the world, and is better than those around him. As far as he is concerned, he never has to prove this superiority; it just *is*. He automatically is more important than you just by virtue of being him. He may never have earned it, and you may actually have proven yourself to be the better athlete, employee, artist, or anything else, but he will absolutely assert that he is more important.

Along with this belief of superiority, grandiosity comes with a certain level of infallibility as well. The narcissist believes he cannot be at fault for anything, or that he is invincible. Even when his behavior is clearly in the wrong to everyone looking in at the situation, he refuses to admit or believe that he could be the problem. It always lies with someone else.

This behavior can be as seemingly innocent as denying blame in an argument, citing the other person's behavior as the real cause for everything, or as delusional as insisting that some outside source, such as a big patch of ice was the real reason he ran into a building and not the fact that he had chosen to have a few drinks before leaving. He insists that the problem was not with him and his choices or behaviors, but rather with the world around him or the people he interacted with.

A preoccupation with fantasies of unlimited success, power, brilliance, beauty, or love

Because the narcissist believes she is superior, she believes she is entitled to perfection, riches, or power and obsesses over these ideals. She dreams of a grand life, filled with fortune, beauty, the perfect romantic partner, and anything else she ever could desire. Despite her expectations being impossible for the average person, she wholeheartedly fixates on them. Anything that falls short of her expectations will either face her wrath or be discarded while she continues her conquest.

Unfortunately for the narcissist, nothing in this world is as perfect as she believes, and her grandiose beliefs and fantasies are perpetually challenged and proven false. Ultimately, the narcissist never feels satisfied, despite her best effort to attain everything she believes she deserves simply by virtue of being a perfect person.

This preoccupation with having something better at all times is why, in relationships, narcissists often begin demanding more and more from their partners, and nothing you ever do is good enough for them. They want more from you than you will ever be able to provide, and once you acknowledge that desire they possess is for an impossible standard, the weight of trying to be good enough for them begins to diminish.

A belief of uniqueness

The idea that he is superior in all ways also lends itself to many narcissists believing they are unique or special. This uniqueness comes with the added burden of being misunderstood by all the so-called commoners that surround him. His uniqueness comes with a higher social status than the people around him have attained, and those who have not reached his higher status cannot possibly understand how he thinks or why he does what he does.

To the narcissist, this uniqueness is the perfect excuse to disregard other people's dissent. Since those around him disagree, they are clearly not the same status as him, and therefore their opinions are unimportant. He has no reason to pay attention to the opinions of the uneducated. After all, a neurosurgeon would never take advice from a burger flipper on how to perform a surgery; the burger flipper almost definitely does not have years and years of experience in the medical field, and therefore, his opinion on a technique would be irrelevant and likely misguided.

Unwilling to admit mediocrity, the narcissist exhibiting this behavior oftentimes tells those around him that they do not know what they are talking about, or they do not understand genius. He likely refuses to associate with certain people or brands, worried about how it would reflect on him if he were ever caught inside a commoner's store like Walmart.

The narcissist believes his specialness qualifies him to be an expert in everything, and also as a weapon when he needs to be a victim. No one else has it as bad as he does, and if they do, then they obviously do not have the same problems he does for some other reason. If someone else's mother has passed away, the narcissist is quick to chime in that his entire family died in a car crash when he was young. If someone else is struggling with schoolwork, he had it worse because he had to work full time and study, and while he is doing this, he is attending a much more rigorous university. The uniqueness or specialness is not limited to superiority; the narcissist is just as quick to be the ultimate victim in the story as he is to be the ultimate protagonist protected by the shield of plot armor if that will feed his ego.

A need for excessive or constant admiration

Narcissists, in a sense, are addicted to admiration, or at the very least, attention. True to addict behavior, the narcissist often does anything to draw attention her way. If she can, she often prefers to get it positively, through seeking careers that lend themselves to attention and public spotlight, or are powerful, such as doctors, politicians, police officers, or teachers. Each of these offers a steady stream of *narcissistic supply*, which is the attention narcissists crave.

In the event that working for narcissistic supply is too difficult or impossible, narcissists will just as quickly turn to the victim role in order to garner sympathy. They will suddenly have a gravely ill family member, or may even claim to be terminally ill themselves, or they will create a situation that makes them vulnerable so others will rescue them, such as drinking too much, or even resorting to causing an injury that is not quite bad enough to be serious, but is enough to cause others to stop and help them.

The narcissist's insatiable craving for attention and admiration drives them to suddenly announce their own engagement at their best friend's bridal shower, or worse, their wedding reception. The attention must always somehow shift back to the narcissist any time it is not on her.

A sense of entitlement

Along with his delusion of grandeur, the narcissist believes that he deserves whatever he wants specifically because he wants it. Rather than having to earn affection, attention, money, power, or anything else in his life, he expects it to be handed to him on a silver platter. While the average person must earn respect, power, and money, and may feel entitled to them after going through the effort of earning them, the narcissist prefers to skip the earning stage. He demands it all with none of the effort.

For example, a narcissist may feel entitled to a perfect score on an exam even though he barely studied. When he gets his test results that reflect his effort accordingly, he may painstakingly go through and challenge every point his professor made, attempting to justify why his wrong answer could technically be right. Likewise, a boss may expect respect from his employees, even though he has done nothing to earn it other than wearing the title of boss. He feels entitled to it, even though he may actually treat his employees like garbage.

Exploitative or manipulative behavior

As people with unrealistic goals and expectations, it should be unsurprising that narcissists are also master manipulators. Even the person they present to everyone around them is a lie created through manipulative techniques such as mirroring and projecting. On top of lying about who they are at a fundamental level, narcissists also manipulate those around them to give them what they want, even if that manipulation comes at a serious cost. They often hide this manipulative behavior behind a veil of plausible deniability, enabling them to deny any time they are called out for manipulating.

Oftentimes, the narcissist will deny any claim of fault, such as denying he is cheating on his partner when he really is carrying on an affair. Immediately after, he attacks his partner, claiming that she is delusional and insecure because of previous relationship experience, and immediately after, reversing the claim, accusing her of being the one cheating and projecting onto him. This manipulative behavior puts his partner on the defensive, derailing her accusation and shifting the focus from his behavior to hers, and she now feels that the onus is on her to prove she is innocent.

A lack of empathy

Lacking empathy makes manipulating others much easier, so it is no surprise that a manipulative individual may also lack the capacity for empathy. Empathy has a key point in the survival of humanity; without being able to empathize, we would struggle to make sure our social group is cared for because we would have little reason or motivation to care about their wellbeing. Empathy helps us not only care for those around us but also shows us when not to cross boundaries and when to give each other space to defuse conflicts.

Without this empathetic connection to others, the narcissist does not care about their feelings. He understands how they feel on a superficial level, but seeing someone in pain does not make him feel bad or sympathetic for that person. Likewise, seeing the teenage cashier break down into tears at the store after he berates her does not make him feel guilt that cues him to stop.

Instead, he sees an opportunity to feel powerful and in control of the situation, which feeds his ego, and he continues goading her.

Envious of others, or expectant that others are envious of him or her

Since the narcissist feels entitled to anything she desires, and also has an obsession with perfection, whenever she sees someone that has what she wants but does not have, she cannot help but feel envious. Someone who was chosen for a promotion she wanted will not be congratulated, and may even find their accomplishment minimized by the narcissist instead. She may even manage to spin the minimizing in such a way that she instead convinces herself that the other person should be envious of her instead. After all, that promotion came with such a small boost in pay but had so many more responsibilities. She convinces herself that she would have turned down the promotion if it had been offered to her because it was not the right fit at all.

Presents as arrogant or haughty

The last of the nine traits that present in NPD is a haughty or arrogant disposition. Since the narcissist believes he is superior, he often acts as such with little regard for the feelings of others. Those who are not his superior or equal are less than him and therefore do not deserve basic respect or human decency. After all, they are only there to serve him if they are beneath him, and it is not serving him if he is busy pandering to their delicate feelings. If they wanted to be treated better, he believes, they should have done more with themselves than work a job in a service profession.

The saying that you can tell a lot about a person by how he treats the waiter on a date rings true here; the narcissist will likely jump at the opportunity to belittle or upset the waiters, and then use the fact that the waiters are upset, to begin with, to negotiate some sort of discount or special treatment from management. If the waiter dares to say anything in defense of himself, the narcissist may snap back that he is paying the waiter's bills by virtue of being in the restaurant, and the waiter needs to learn his place and remember that the customer is always right.

CHAPTER 2

Everyday Narcissism

Oftentimes when people realize they are facing a narcissist, they feel the need to ask themselves why. Why do narcissists behave the way they do? What do they gain by doing so? Do they choose to be this way? The short answer is not usually: Narcissism as we know it is a personality disorder. It is caused by a series of disordered thoughts and irrational behaviors that affect the narcissist's ability to understand the world around her. Answering why the narcissist behaves the way she does requires a much longer answer, but at its simplest, there are three common reasons for narcissists to behave narcissistically: As a coping mechanism, as a reaction to a perceived threat, and due to cognitive distortions born from the previous two reasons.

Narcissism as a Coping Mechanism

Nobody likes to feel like they lack control over a situation. Being at the mercy of someone else, fate, or strangers with no connections to you is terrifying, even for those of us without distorted thinking or personality disorders. For the narcissist, that lack of control is absolutely devastating; he thrives on being in control and making sure his expectations are adhered to and meet his standards. This fear is so overwhelming that he feels the need to develop methods to avoid it at all costs. He needs to have control over himself or his situation, or he risks spiraling into a depression of negative feelings.

Oftentimes, for the narcissist, this fear of lack of control over his situation is due to some sort of trauma or neglect during childhood. He lacked the control to protect himself as a child, so he now seeks to seize control of everything within his reach, grasping at any opportunities to influence what happens around him in a sort of coping mechanism. It is his way to ensure that he is never at the mercy of someone else's control in order to protect himself. In his mind, by always being in control, no one is ever in a position to hurt him. After all, a position of power is one of the most dangerous to those beneath him.

The trauma we face as children never gets processed the way we process trauma as adults; children lack the skills we learn through growing up with someone there to help guide us through navigating through trauma and stress, and oftentimes, the trauma is repressed until later, when it eventually exhibits in different ways. The abused child may grow up to be fearful of all conflict, even if he does not remember the actual abuse. The sounds of even a polite argument could send him into a panic if that was a trigger from childhood. For the narcissist, the neglect or abuse was likely emotional; his caregivers were likely unavailable when he needed them, or may have belittled everything he did and made him feel unworthy and guilty about not being good enough. Because of this, he develops a fear of criticism and powerlessness at an early age. Despite his best efforts, he felt like he was never good enough to get his parents' attention and affection, and because of this, he quickly began to believe that he was not good enough. After all, if he were, then his parents would have been much more interested in interacting with him. Regardless of whether the abuse was through angry words spewed at him, degrading him and wearing away his self-esteem or through ignoring his emotional needs and being an absent parent, the result is the same: A child who has deeply internalized that he is not good enough and has built his entire personality and perceptions of the world atop that assumption. Just as a skyscraper built on a crooked, cracked foundation will never support the weight of the whole building, the narcissist's personality's foundation is incapable of bearing the weight of normal, day-to-day adult stressors

Over time, the child's mindset shifts to one more reminiscent of a narcissist than is typically expected of a child; he may become hyper-focused on perfection, or tell himself that he is better than everyone else as a way to cope with feeling inadequate. By maintaining a façade of perfection, he tries to avoid any sort of backlash. He feels as though he cannot be criticized if he manages to maintain a perfect image, protecting his fragile ego from further damage. The child grows up and never manages to get past that way of thinking. He is still obsessed with perfection or convincing himself that he is special in some way, shape, or form, except now he is an adult, and it is no longer within normal behavior standards. His coping mechanisms to deal with a lack of control are not considered normal behavior, and those around him may judge him harshly if they catch him in the act of such childish behavior, something he also desperately fears. Humiliation and degradation are the worst pain someone can inflict upon him, and because of this, he oftentimes hides his behaviors as best as he can. Ultimately, however, these behaviors are coping mechanisms, and under significant pressure or feeling as if he is spiraling out of control, he may snap and lash out, or even intentionally hurt whoever he deemed the cause of his powerlessness. By hurting the one without power, he has, in his own distorted way, asserted that he is, in fact, in control over the person who sought to steal his power. After all, if he were not in control, at least at some superficial level, he would not have been able to cause the person pain. Even only having power over someone's pain is enough for him to feel justified in his control over the situation, despite the cost of potentially ruining a relationship or severing a connection with someone who may have been useful to the narcissist in the future.

Narcissism as a Reaction to a Threat

The lack of control the narcissist has over the situation and world around her, being the narcissist's biggest fear, means that she is constantly in a state of reacting. Every time any control is perceived to be out of her hands is seen as a threat that needs to be neutralized. The narcissist seeks to gain that control back by any means necessary, even if that involves manipulation, coercion, or even abuse. Narcissists will rely on whatever tactics they have in their toolbox to get their control, even if it is morally wrong or causes pain. The narcissist does not empathize with others and has no reason to not manipulate her way into power if that is how she gets what she wants and protects her fragile ego from harm.

For some, this will be as simple as manipulating the situation and becoming the faultless victim. They make it so nothing negative is their own fault, which allows them to avoid whatever control they cannot have from hurting them. People will not usually harass or demean the victim, so if she cannot outwardly be in control and powerful, she will skillfully manipulate the situation. This is a sort of power in and of itself; even though she takes the role of the powerless, blameless victim, she is still in control by virtue of being able to skew the perceptions of everyone around her.

Sometimes, the narcissist seeks to gain outward control and puts on a façade of importance, confidence, and intelligence that allows her to gain a legitimate following. People naturally defer to the charismatic, intelligent leader that knows exactly what to do and always seems to present with an air of perfection. By creating this persona, the narcissist gains power in careers or communities, earning higher positions that fulfill her need for control and power. She cannot feel threatened when she is in a position of power, neutralizing the threats of powerlessness. By earning respect in the community, she is automatically regarded with the respect she desires, and by having manipulated herself to that position in the first place, she satisfies her desire for control.

Sometimes, narcissists use abusive, coercive tactics to exert control. They browbeat those around them into giving them whatever they want. They will demean, belittle, and manipulate if that is what it takes to get their control. They are so afraid of losing their position they perceive to be invulnerable that they will hurt those around them to maintain it. They are able to do this by first building rapport with another person and then systematically tearing them down, little by little until they leave behind someone so utterly broken and defeated that they are easily controlled. The narcissist's victim, in this case, is oftentimes someone close to her, either a romantic partner or a family member, and she will completely convince her victim that he or she is incapable of anything without her power or influence. Oftentimes, the threat perceived from family members is the threat that they will leave and therefore control the pace of the relationship. The narcissist cannot accept that someone other than she would be able to make decisions on if or when the relationship ends or what pace it will take and she seeks to destroy the other person's ability or desire to leave. This does not necessarily mean that she wants to maintain the relationship, however; she will have zero qualms overthrowing her victim to the side and never contacting him or her again if that is what she desires to do.

For the narcissist, so long as she perceives she is in control and unchallenged, she will likely be relatively harmless. However, challenging that control can have explosive results. Just as she reacted strongly to the perception of a threat of powerlessness, she will react strongly to any threat of her claim of power. She will feel like any criticism must immediately be crushed in order to discourage anyone from attempting it again, and will become belligerent if she feels that is the only way to protect herself. A challenged narcissist can be dangerous, as they will lash out with every ounce of vitriol in their body in order to beat everyone back into line and complacency, leaving her sitting atop her throne of manipulation rather than forcing her to face her shattered sense of self head-on.

Narcissistic Distortions

The lies that the narcissist tries to perpetuate are his own deeply-held beliefs. In order to cope with the traumas of childhood, he has literally rewritten the narrative on his life in order to benefit himself. The irony of the narcissist is that he is so afraid of losing control and exposure that he has even manipulated himself into believing the lies he spins. He has inadvertently given over control out of fear of acknowledging his lack of power by clouding his own judgment to the point that he is no longer able to see the world for what it is. He is so preoccupied with attempting to protect himself that he has lied to even himself about what has happened to him.

The narcissist has convinced himself wholeheartedly that the persona he projects and his revisionist history are accurate, which is part of the reason he gets so defensive when it is challenged. To challenge his control, his actions, or his legitimacy is to challenge his fragilely constructed persona and his deeply held beliefs of what is happening and what has happened in the past. Like a glass sculpture, it will only take one or two major cracks before the entire persona comes crashing down.

Just how you may have beliefs that you are devout about believing and learning that that belief was fault would leave you devastated, the narcissist would be utterly destroyed if he felt as if those beliefs were proven wrong. Those are fundamental parts of the personality he has tried to piece together with all of the broken shards of his ego, and cracking that would mean that he has to admit that he himself is a lie. The person he thought he was is a lie. That is a devastating realization to grapple with for those of us with healthy coping mechanisms. For the narcissist who lacks these healthy ways to deal with stress, it is far too excruciating to even acknowledge, so he lives firmly in denial. Rather than dealing with the lies he is weaving and correcting them while they are still small, he instead sits in the middle, continuing to weave the lies to sustain the original ones as he grows more and more entangled, insisting everything is fine. Eventually, all that remains is a knotted mess in the center of the web, unrecognizable as what the narcissist may have become, given a chance. The truth becomes so deeply buried that the narcissist would have no way to discover it without completely and utterly destroying the web that he has created and everything that has been built atop of it. This could be careers, marriages, wealth, and connections that he has only gotten out of his pretense of being the persona he created.

Instead of doing the morally right thing and being truthful, he continues to build delusions and narratives that support his own perception of the truth. He becomes so obsessed with justifying his own delusions to others that he sees no other option but to believe them. The truth is so convoluted and entangled at that point that it is impossible to see, so there is no going back. It is easier to move forward than it is to try to disentangle everything. Eventually, what is left is a persona built with lie upon lie on a fragile, cracking foundation. The narcissist does what he can to defend this distorted personality he has created, and it often means relying on narcissistic behavior to do so. He has to lie and manipulate others, so they believe his perspective. He has to control others, so he does not risk them going out of their way to prove him wrong and send the entire thing shattering. He has to project onto others as a distorted way of coping with his own complicated feelings of self-loathing and broken self-esteem. He feels the need to hurt others to feel as if he has gained control of a situation he deemed as spiraling out of control.

Each of these narcissistic behaviors is done in order to protect the persona he created at the center of it all and prevent it from shattering and leaving the real him standing in the middle of the wreckage, exposed for all to see. All of it is to protect that fragile self he has invented to shield himself from emotional harm as a child. The delusional self he created as a child feels like the only thing between himself and the constant threats of the outside world, and the only thing holding that persona together is an ever-growing web of lies and manipulations he spins. Ultimately, his intense drive for self-preservation is more powerful than his drive for anything else, so he will say anything necessary to maintain his delusions.

CHAPTER 3

Secret Feelings

Despite how narcissists tend to present themselves, full of charisma and confidence, on the inside is typically a broken, wounded individual with no true sense of self. The narcissist never had the chance to develop a normal, healthy. While some narcissists' lack of sense of self is turned into a true, deeply held belief of superiority, many others are much more vulnerable. This is even a recognized kind of narcissism: Vulnerable narcissism, in which the narcissist feels inadequate and insecure and overcompensates with the grandiosity, tendency to manipulate, and creating a persona of the perfect victim that is never to blame for anything. These narcissists are overwhelmed with all sorts of secret feelings they aim to hide from public view at all costs, though their mask will fall under extreme stress or emotion.

Identity Crisis

Insecurity and vulnerability are at the foundation of many narcissists. Whether due to abuse during childhood or some other trauma, the narcissist has internalized that insecurity. Where most people have a voice that regulates their sense of self-worth, telling them that they are good enough and keeping them comfortable in their own skin, the narcissist hears a voice telling her she is inadequate. Nothing she ever does is good enough for her, and she constantly hears her inner voice putting her down. She constantly feels insecure in her own skin and humiliated that she feels the way she does. The idea that other people can see how insecure she really is horrifies the narcissist because she feels as if that admission of insecurity is an admission of weakness and that the voices that shaped her own poor sense of self-worth were correct. Other people acknowledging her insecurity makes her vulnerable, as that would be the easiest target to further humiliate and degrade her the first time she makes a mistake.

That inner voice we all hear is created by our parents or primary caregivers; the way our caregivers speak to us becomes the way we speak to ourselves. When our caregivers are overly critical, harsh, or cruel, their disapproval and loathing become internalized. We believe their word because, as children, we are hardwired to defer to our caregivers. We instinctively trust their judgments as correct because it is their jobs to help us learn to navigate through the world. The parent's role in a child's life is to teach the child how to be successful, well-adjusted, and all the skills he or she will need in order to cope with all of the turmoil that comes with being an adult. Some parents fail miserably, sometimes due to their own abuse or just through lacking the empathy and parental instincts required to be a successful parent. When parents constantly criticize or put down their child, their words become the child's frame for seeing the world around her.

When the child hears nothing but negativity and sees the world in that negative mindset, her entire way of thinking changes. She becomes insecure about everything, constantly feeling incompetent and vulnerable. Her entire sense of self is shameful, negative, and self-loathing. With that loathing sense of self, she feels the need to overcompensate, and her behaviors become standoffish. She creates a persona focused on herself, pretending to be perfect, faultless, and likable in order to combat these feelings of worthlessness. By presenting as confident and perfect, and convincing others that this is who she is, she is able to protect herself from the scathing words she has come to expect from herself and others. She is even able to sometimes convince herself that she is as confident and fantastic as she presents to those around her, though she frequently swings right back to feeling insecure and vulnerable a short time later. Living in this nearly permanent state of insecurity leaves the narcissist constantly feeling defensive and on edge, unable to relax for fear of someone around her taking advantage of her vulnerability and using it to climb the social hierarchy.

Issues with Intimacy

The intense levels of shame these narcissists feel act as deterrents from any real intimacy or relationships. Intimacy requires vulnerability that the narcissist seeks to avoid at all costs, and therefore, it is avoided. The narcissist refuses to become vulnerable others, seeking instead to protect her fragile ego from harm. She recognizes that being vulnerable means risking her ego being harmed, and that is not a risk she is willing to take. Vulnerability requires trust, and the narcissist will not trust anyone but herself. She knows that as soon as she makes herself vulnerable, she risks having the shame and self-loathing she feels confirmed and validated by the person she emotionally exposed herself to, and she refuses to risk that. Her fragile ego would not be able to take any sort of criticism from someone she trusted, so instead, she decides to avoid trusting anyone at all.

Despite the fact that narcissists are emotionally stunted, they are typically quite intelligent and do recognize that there is a relationship between trust and vulnerability. Recognizing that trust and vulnerability are required for an intimate relationship, the narcissist instead decides not to commit. The relationship does not seem worthwhile enough, and the promise of intimacy is not enough for the narcissist to intentionally render herself vulnerable to someone else. Remember, her narcissistic behaviors are a coping mechanism to make herself invulnerable to harm; it would be counterproductive to go out of her way to become vulnerable, regardless of the reason. At the root of refusing to become vulnerable is the shame and self-loathing that underlies all of her behaviors. She fears being humiliated, berated, or harmed again, and that fear makes a connection with others quite difficult. True intimacy is never achieved with the narcissist because of her narcissistic nature's existence as a coping mechanism, although she will pretend and go through the motions of being in a relationship if she sees the benefit of doing so. It is important to remember, though, that she will never truly trust her partner and will never really make herself emotionally available or exposed.

Self-Direction and Deflection

While nobody enjoys being humiliated or embarrassed, narcissists fear humiliation more than anything else. Because narcissists already have impossible standards set for themselves and they already see themselves as broken and fragile, to have someone else make them feel that way feels like salt in the wound. Knowing how fragile they really are and fearing that fragility being exposed, narcissists seek to avoid humiliation at all costs.

Because the narcissist fears humiliation, she instead resorts to humiliating others around her. Rather than attempt to address any humiliation on herself, she prefers to insult others, shifting negative attention away from her in ways that leave her blameless, but leave someone else being humiliated. This is another misguided coping mechanism; the narcissist feels too fragile, too self-conscious, and too vulnerable to survive humiliation, so she seeks to instead deflect it to others, even if they were just as undeserving and innocent as the narcissist. This also serves to allow the narcissist to look better in comparison, providing an ego boost where there could have potentially been ego injury.

The narcissist may point out a mistake someone else made, even if it was previously undetected, or even make up a mistake and blame it on someone else in order to keep potential negative attention away from her, even if there was little chance of negative attention being on her in the first place. Oftentimes, she fears humiliation from imagined sources, and that is enough to send her on the defense. The easiest defense to make while maintaining an image of innocence is to force others to be defensive as well. After all, when everyone is behaving defensively, no one is lashing out, and she remains unchallenged.

Undeserving of Empathy

One of the basic tenets of narcissism is the lack of, or diminished capacity for, feeling empathy. This lack of empathy makes it difficult for the narcissist to imagine feeling deserving of empathy. Since empathy is almost foreign to the narcissist after a childhood of never having it emulated for her, she does not consider herself worthy of it, and if she is not worthy, others must not be worthy either. This leaves her thinking the worst of those around her at all times, rather than seeing that many humans are kindhearted and will go out of their way to help due to their empathetic natures. Despite knowing the concept of empathy, it remains utterly foreign to her, and unless she is pretending for a good cause, it will never cross her mind to legitimately be empathetic with someone. Likewise, it would never cross her mind that anyone else would ever treat her with empathy, as even her parents, the two people in the world who are biologically supposed to treat her with empathy and respect, never gave her that courtesy. She must be undeserving if even her parents could not manage to muster up enough care about her to treat her as a human with feelings that deserve to be recognized.

Because of this belief of being unworthy of empathy or kindness, the narcissist views everything as suspicious. Nothing is to be trusted, and every action has an ulterior motive simply because the narcissist always has an ulterior motive. She refuses to see the best in others, and cannot recognize that sometimes people do something out of the kindness of their hearts to selflessly help others because the concept of selflessness is entirely foreign to her. Those behaviors were not modeled for her when they mattered, and she no longer considers them options.

This lack of deserving empathy paired with feelings of worthlessness creates even more feelings of inferiority, as the narcissist does not believe that making a mistake will be treated gracefully or kindly. She is certain that making a mistake is one of the worst-case scenarios, and that it will reflect much worse on her than it actually will. Because of that, she will go to great lengths to hide any mistakes she may make, or push the blame away from herself, using any possible plausible deniability, no matter how realistic or ridiculous her excuse sounds.

Since she is unworthy of that kindness and believes that others will treat her poorly, it becomes easier for her to treat others unkindly instead of empathetically. It is a negative cycle of believing others will treat her poorly because she is unworthy, and therefore, she will treat others that way preemptively to avoid being in a situation of vulnerability. She falls into this habit in order to protect herself and avoid from exerting any energy she could potentially put to better use caring for herself. Since others will not treat her with kindness or help her meet her needs without prompting, she feels driven to force the point and manipulate those around her to get what she feels like she needs or deserves.

CHAPTER 4

The Perfectionism Problem

Narcissists are known perfectionists. They have impossible standards, both for themselves and for others around them. Of course, this creates plenty of opportunities for problems to arise. These perfectionism problems create multiple challenges for the narcissist, who frequently face these expectations of perfection falling short and feeding their feelings of unworthiness or inferiority. When they feel as if they are falling short or feel as if their delusion of perfectionism is teetering on the edge of being shattered, narcissists often react strongly due to their own fragile senses of identity and insecurity that they are hiding behind the perfectionism. When that delusion of perfection is threatened in any way, narcissistic behaviors are more likely to occur for a variety of reasons.

Stress Management

As has been established, narcissism tends to be a coping mechanism. In this context, narcissistic behavior is a way to cope with stress as opposed to a lack of control or insecurity. As people with very rigid expectations of perfection and fragile senses of self, these people struggle with any sort of stress. The narcissist presents himself as perfect and infallible to those around him, and when stressed, he struggles to respond appropriately or on the fly. Stress occurring is typically a major emotional trigger, and his behavior may become volatile and unpredictable. Stress was likely a common theme throughout his childhood, and his ability to deal with stress in a healthy manner never fully developed without proper guidance.

While we know narcissists present themselves as confident, that confidence is a façade. A truly confident person is able to work through stress, even though it is uncomfortable and unpleasant. The narcissist, particularly the vulnerable one, feels an amplified level of stress compared to non-narcissists. A study completed by the University of Michigan psychologist Robin Edelstein[1] measured and tested for stress responses of undergraduate students, and supported that assertion.

During this study, students were told to prepare a presentation to be delivered in front of an audience composed of people who, unknowingly to the presenters, were told not to respond in any way. They were told not to smile, nod, shake their heads, or do anything else acknowledging or reacting to the students. The students were told that the audience was made up of experts of human behavior, though they were random observers. Right before giving the presentations, the researchers took away the presenters' notes and forced them to present from memory to a completely unresponsive audience. The researchers then measured levels of cortisol, the stress hormone, and compared results.

Despite the confidence narcissists present, they showed increased responses to stress, with men rated as more narcissistic displaying higher levels of cortisol, along with worse mood. This result shows narcissists as having much more sensitive negative stress responses compared to non-narcissists, and these results have been replicated in other similar studies as well. The narcissists' fragile egos and true vulnerability they have kept hidden away from everyone betray the persona of confidence they present, and every time something stressful happens, that persona is threatened, or sometimes even shattered.

The narcissist, depending on whether grandiose or vulnerable, will either roll with the stressor or struggle to function. The higher the narcissist's self-esteem, the better he will be able to cope with stress, and grandiose narcissists typically have plenty of self-esteem, as opposed to the vulnerable narcissists, who lack it.

Change Aversion

Similar to expecting perfection, narcissists often feel an intense aversion to change of any kind. Change implies surprises, which typically cause more stress. Their aversion to change only makes them more stressed when change inevitably occurs. The rigidity becomes yet another shortcoming for the narcissist. Oftentimes, this change aversion can actually be used to identify whether someone is a narcissist or not.

When faced with challenges that people can typically take in stride, the narcissist may become triggered and lash out. Something as simple as the store being sold out of an item needed for dinner can cause a meltdown of screaming profanities at the employee that told him she was sorry, but they are sold out at the moment. The stress of being told he has to choose something else is too overwhelming, and he is not afraid of lashing out at other people he sees as at fault.

The narcissist believes he is entitled to exactly what he asked for, and because he is entitled, being told no is a shock. Imagine going to a bank to withdraw some of your money and being told, "No, you can't do that today. The sky is the wrong color, and the wind is blowing the wrong direction, so I'm not giving you your money. Oh, and your cards have been disabled. You'll be able to use it eventually." You would be outraged, and for a good reason. Your money is your own and you bank it with the expectation you are entitled to use it or move it at any time you please; if your bank told you that you were being denied access for an inane reason, you would probably be changing banks at the first opportunity, and most reasonable people would agree.

For the narcissist, anything not going according to plan causes the same level of outraged disbelief, and he reacts as such. The narcissist, with his entitlement combined with his penchant for perfectionism, believes that things will always go his way, even when it is unrealistic. He expects certain things to happen in a certain order, and he feels threatened when that does not happen. Things not going his way is essentially the world challenging his distorted perceptions of the world around him, chipping away bit by bit at his perfect persona. That challenge forces him to come to terms with everything he has worked so hard to bury behind his mask, leaving him once again feeling self-loathing.

In order to cope with those feelings of loathing, he feels the need to redirect that loathing to whoever or whatever is the perceived reason for exploding in the first place. As you may have noticed by now, redirection is one of the narcissist's favorite tactics to avoid blame and explain away any discrepancies in his distorted world. Redirection shifts fault from him, but also allows him to cope with his negative feelings. It becomes a sort of outlet for his frustration; instead of sitting on his frustration and letting it fester, he lets it explode and affect others as well. Misery loves company, and this way, at least he is not the only one miserable, stressed, and frustrated. This allows him to soothe his own fragile ego a little more, reminding himself that the other people around him are equally as outraged, even though the other people are more frustrated about the narcissist's behavior than whatever happened.

The Perfectionism Problem

Falling Short

Another common problem also entails from this misguided perfectionism: Constantly failing to meet expectations. While those around him see the narcissist as harsh, unrealistic, and overly demanding, he is even harder on himself. He knows that the people around him are not perfect; that is part of how he justifies his own superiority. He expects himself to be perfect and presents himself as such to hide his fragile self-worth in a misguided attempt to push those feelings of insufficiency away.

Unfortunately, perfection is something that only exists in theory. Humans are perfectly imperfect, and that imperfection that so many of us embrace as the beauty of humanity is seen as nothing more than a flaw that ruins the image for the narcissist. If it is not flawless, it is not valuable or worthwhile, and he holds himself to that standard as well. Flaws and weaknesses do not develop character; they are hindrances. Hindrances cause us to make mistakes, which cause blame, which lead to humiliation and shame.

This perceived spiral into shame is something the narcissist seeks to desperately avoid. With humiliation being feared more than anything else, the narcissist instead attempts to create perfection to create something invulnerable to criticism. Unfortunately, this is counterproductive, as the narcissist has now created an unattainable goal, which will inevitably lead to the humiliation of falling short that he so desperately sought to avoid.

When failing, narcissists are prone to spirals into either rage or depression, and at that moment, *narcissistic injury* occurs. Narcissistic injury refers to threats to the narcissist's self-esteem or that challenge the narcissist's delusional perception of reality. The narcissist's reaction to narcissistic injury is visceral; the narcissist responds in such a way that those around him may think he is fighting for his life as he flies into a narcissistic rage, and in some ways, he is. He is fighting to protect that carefully constructed persona that has become his life. He cannot let that mask slip without admitting that he has been fake the entire time. The narcissist's reaction to other people's failure is often disproportionate to the perceived crime, ranging from a silent treatment to screaming, or even hurting the source of injury in an attempt to make it disappear.

The reason for this visceral reaction is a way to shift from feeling like the victim to being in control of the situation.

It is a method of self-soothing, albeit a poor one. By reestablishing himself as dominant by inflicting pain on others, he is able to feel as if he is in control and like the world is in line with his perceptions once again. If he cannot be in control of his own perfection because that is an impossible idealistic standard to achieve, he can at least be in control of those around him who fail.

Dealing with a Narcissist

SECTION 2

Engaging the Narcissist

CHAPTER 5

Therapeutic Approaches

Approaching correcting narcissistic personality disorder or narcissistic tendencies can be quite daunting; after all, narcissists' façade of perfection means they can never admit fault with their behavior. Even if they do, their proclivity to rage when they feel challenged or threatened in any way makes it difficult to work with narcissists that are willing to begin the process of developing a whole, healthy self that they currently lack. Narcissists tend to react poorly to change, being challenged, and failure, all of which are present during therapy to correct narcissistic behaviors. Between their inability to admit fault and their tendency to avoid change, treating narcissists becomes incredibly difficult, and narcissists that are willing to go through that ordeal are quite rare. However, when a narcissist or someone exhibiting narcissistic behaviors is ready to begin changing or admits that different behaviors would be more beneficial, schema-focused therapy is one of the most effective methods of treatment.

What are Schema-Focused Approaches?

Schema-focused therapy is a type of psychotherapy, or talk therapy, that combines some of the key features of cognitive behavioral therapy, experiential therapy, and interpersonal therapy together to create an entirely new approach in order to treat various personality disorders. This therapy is based on identifying which schemas, or patterns of negative behaviors that a person repeats. Schema-focused therapy has been found to be beneficial for those with self-defeating schemas that do not respond well to other kinds of psychotherapy, making it sound quite promising for narcissists.

In this therapy, it is believed that negative schemas cause destructive thinking and that those destructive schemas are developed during adolescence through experience and

Therapeutic Approaches

treatment by family. As you will recall, narcissists tend to internalize criticism they heard growing up, and therefore, they should be a good fit for schema-focused therapy when they are willing to cooperate. Schema-focused therapy occurs in three steps: The therapist identifying schemas, the client discovering his or her own schemas, and correcting the schemas as they are relevant in real life situations.

The first step involves the therapist identifying whatever schemas the narcissist is trapped in. This involves conversations with the narcissist to delve into the narcissist's past and plenty of discussions on motivations. The therapist may listen to what the narcissist has to say and ask guiding or clarifying questions in order to begin to develop an idea of the narcissist's personality and why he behaves the way he does. Through training, the therapist learns to identify which aspects of the conversation may be relevant to the narcissist's behavior, even if what is being discussed at the moment and the narcissist's behavior seem entirely unrelated.

The second step involves the therapist helping the narcissist begin to identify her schemas. By learning what they are, they are then prepared to begin identifying when they occur in everyday life. The purpose of this is that being aware of the schemas and being able to identify them in real time allows for the narcissist to correct the behaviors in real time. This is achieved through various forms of role-playing, imagery, and any other techniques the therapist may find useful for that particular client. At this point, the therapist is guiding the narcissist to come to the conclusion of why they act the way they do, with the hopes of understanding their behaviors more in-depth and recognizing why they are harmful.

The third step involves improving thinking patterns in the real world in real time and replacing negative, distorted, or unhealthy thoughts with healthy, productive, and positive ones for positive results. This is a key facet of cognitive behavioral therapy, in which by recognizing the relationship between thoughts, feelings, and actions, you seek to alter your actions by changing your thoughts. If you change a negative thought into a positive one, your feelings on the subject will also become more positive as well. When you are in a positive mindset, you are more likely to behave positively in return.

Maladaptive Schemas

One of the most fundamental concepts in schema therapy is maladaptive schemas. By understanding a schema as a pervasive pattern of behavior, we can then identify a

Therapeutic Approaches

maladaptive schema as a negative pattern of behavior, oftentimes developed some time during childhood. Maladaptive schemas are the results of an upbringing that made developing a normal, healthy sense of self and behavior difficult or impossible. By not having basic emotional needs met by the parent or caregiver, the child compensates by falling into these schemas in order to meet the need the best he or she can. They are deemed maladaptive coping mechanisms to the many stressors the world throws at us.

Since we learn these schemas early in life, they are all we know. For the narcissist, or for others with maladaptive schemas, these thoughts have been present for as long as they can remember, and therefore are familiar. As creatures of habits, we automatically seek out the familiar and comfortable, no matter how dangerous it may be. This is why we often see people who grew up with dysfunctional families falling victim to dysfunctional relationships in adulthood. It becomes a cycle of the person not knowing any different, and seeking it out for themselves in adulthood. To the one with the maladaptive schemas, this is the way of life, and that is accepted.

The problem with this, however, is that the narcissist begins to distort his perceptions of reality in order to force them to fit into the schemas he has developed. If the narcissist expects the square to fit in the circle spot in a puzzle, it is easier for him to cut off the corners and edges to force it into place than it is for him to accept the truth. If the narcissist develops a pattern of thought in which he is always the victim, he will always twist situations around to make himself the victim even when he is the true antagonizer. This can make things especially difficult when dealing with a narcissist, because he may truly believe that he is the victim when he has been calling you names all day, or blame you for his bad behavior, citing that he would never have done what he did if you had never upset him.

These schemas may remain hidden away the majority of the time, only triggered by certain experiences or situations. This can make discovering which maladaptive schemas a narcissist has difficult, as it can be hard to unbury them all if nothing relevant to the hidden schemas comes up during the identifying stage of therapy. Luckily, this therapy is a longer-term intervention, sometimes lasting upwards of three years, so there will be plenty of time to identify even the most hidden of schemas.

Therapeutic Approaches

Informing Patterns of Thinking

Ultimately, the core intervention in schema therapy aims to reduce the prevalence of the maladaptive schemas and behaviors associated with them in order to reduce the problem behaviors. It does this by focusing on the origin of the maladaptive schemas. By knowing where they came from, the therapist can help the narcissist begin to correct the behavior. Knowing that the schemas were developed due to unmet needs, the therapist seeks to help the patient navigate through his thoughts on those unmet needs and begin to remove the negative connotations and try to meet them now as an adult. The idea is to help the patient create a healthy adult mindset that is prepared and capable of handling stress without falling into old habits of maladaptive schemas and behaviors.

The therapist will try to guide the narcissist through his childhood, typically first starting by asking how his childhood was and how his relationships with his parents were before delving into anything that may be relevant to the behaviors. For example, if the narcissist tends to be hyper-focused on perfection at all times, the therapist may search for signs of his parents being controlling or completely disengaged from their child's life. It is possible that the narcissist is so perfectionistic because his parents were strict to the point that he would be punished for anything less than perfection, or that his parents were so uninterested in him that he overcompensated by trying to be perfect in order to earn their attention.

Neither overly controlling nor negligent and uninterested are healthy parenting styles that meet a child's emotional needs, so it would be no surprise that a child who grew up with a helicopter parent or with little supervision would have some emotional scars. Unable to learn how to cope properly with stress or failure, the narcissist instead lashes out at the possibility of failure, no matter how small. Even something as innocuous as spilling some milk when pouring it into a bowl of cereal could set the narcissist off.

Once the trigger for the schema has been identified, the therapist seeks to identify the cause. Through asking questions and guiding the conversation, it may come to light that the narcissist's own parents were harsh whenever he made normal messes that would be expected from children, and they would punish him for spilling his milk or leaving crumbs on the table. Over time, the child would develop an aversion to anything short of perfection and would get to the point of reacting strongly when not living up to those standards.

Therapeutic Approaches

By understanding that the narcissist's parents were the cause of the behavior of obsessive perfectionism, the therapist would seek to heal the intensity of emotions associated with that particular instance. By slowly changing how the narcissist feels about the incident, the narcissist's own reaction should change as well, which should begin to correct and replace maladaptive schemas with adaptive, healthy behaviors. This change in feelings associated with the memory is done with three types of techniques: cognitive, experiential, and behavioral, as well as with what is known in schema therapy as limited reparenting. Each of these serves a different purpose and has a different use in healing from schemas.

Cognitive strategies take parts of cognitive behavioral therapy and apply them to the narcissist's schema. They may take the form of pros and cons lists, in which the narcissist is asked to make a list of pros and cons of his behaviors in hopes of seeing that there are far more cons than pros. This also may involve testing the validity of a schema, which requires the narcissist to reflect on it and identify how true it really is, or if it is distorted or negative. By identifying it as distorted or negative, it is flagged as needing to be repaired.

Experiential strategies draw from Gestalt psychodrama and imagery techniques. Psychodrama is a form of roleplaying where the patient dramatizes his own life and behavior in order to gain insight about their behaviors and thoughts. It requires a protagonist that is facing a certain problem, such as when the narcissist spilled milk as a child. The narcissist is then asked to reenact the scene of spilling the milk. The reenactment may include soliloquies, where the acting client is told to speak his thoughts as they are happening in character, in order to gain insight into his mental state. This allows for the narcissist to deepen his emotional development and understanding of his own behaviors that have been largely unconscious until that point.

Behavioral strategies draw from traditional behavior therapy such as roleplaying an interaction during therapy, then being expected to execute that interaction in real life in real time before the next meeting. This seeks to teach the narcissist how the proper interaction should go between two healthy individuals, then expects the narcissist to execute it himself. This provides the tools necessary without hand-holding.

Limited reparenting is one of the core features of schema therapy. Knowing that schema therapy assumes that a child with unmet emotional needs develops maladaptive schemas, it seems intuitive to believe that by meeting those needs now, the maladaptive behavior can be corrected. Limited reparenting involves establishing a secure attachment to the therapist, with clear boundaries to keep the relationship appropriate between professional and patient. The therapist does what he or she can in order to meet the needs of the client that went unmet through childhood. This secure attachment allows the client to begin learning to function in a healthy way.

Just a Friendly Reminder...

I'd like to offer you this amazing resource which my clients pay for. It is a report I written when I first began my journey.

Click on the picture above or navigate to the website below to join my exclusive email list. Upon joining, you will receive this incredible report on how to recognize an abusive relationship.

If you ask most people on the street what an abusive relationship is, chances are you'd get a description of physical abuse. And yes, that is most certainly an abusive relationship. However, abuse comes in many forms. The actual meaning of abuse is when someone exerts control over another person.

Find out more about recognizing an abusive relationship and learn how to take control over your life by clicking on the book above or by going to this link:

http://bit.ly/RecognizeAbusiveRelationship

CHAPTER 6

Assessment & Identification

Throughout the course of schema therapy, Dr. Jeff Young, the creator of schema therapy, identified eighteen common maladaptive schemas[2] that may be encountered. Any combination of any number of these can be present at any given time in an individual, and any number of them can influence behavior in negative ways. Understanding these maladaptive schemas will help you recognize that the narcissist may not mean to cause the toxic behavior she exhibits and will give you ideas on how to better deal with the narcissist in a way that defuses the situation instead of causing it to explode.

Recognizing Schemas

The eighteen schemas can be easily divided into five categories for ease of organization and understanding. These categories are disconnection or rejection, impaired autonomy or performance, impaired limits, other-directedness, and over-vigilance or inhibition. Each of these can be recognized as traits of narcissist personality disorder: Narcissists fear rejection and humiliation, they believe they are entitled, they often play the victim, they are impulsive, and they often obsess over other people, whether for their attention or to control them. Understanding the various schemas behind each of these behaviors can help you not only empathize with the narcissist but also help you learn how to interact with her in the healthiest way possible. Particularly when you want to maintain a relationship with a narcissist at any level, understanding these schemas and using your knowledge of the schemas to guide your own behaviors will help you begin to interact with the narcissist in a much more productive, healthy way.

Disconnection/Rejection

Abandonment

Those who have developed a schema of abandonment fear the end of relationships. Oftentimes, they feel disposable and that their partners are likely to toss them aside, whether due to conflict or disagreeing on something mundane, such as what shows to watch before bed or what their favorite restaurants are. Sometimes, they also fear that death, divorce, affairs, or fights, are all inevitably there to end the relationship because of past experiences. While death will eventually take us all, they worry that it will come too soon, or if they let themselves get attached. They assume that they are unworthy of relationships and that anyone who does want them must have some sort of issue or they would go out of their way to choose a more suitable partner.

Mistrust

People who find themselves stuck in the mistrust schema fear being hurt by others, either physically or emotionally. They fear being lied to or betrayed and worry about those around them being out to get them. Ultimately, the fear of being betrayed or hurt leaves them constantly doubting the people around them and latching onto any signs that their friends or loved ones are out to get them. Even an innocent mistake, such as forgetting that the mistrustful individual absolutely despises tomatoes and serving spaghetti, and a garden salad with grape tomatoes mixed in at a large dinner party would be deemed an attack on the person with the end goal being to tell the mistrustful one that her friend hates her and wants her to feel unwelcome and uncomfortable at group events. Accidents are deemed passive aggressive and intentional, and ultimately, the person's ability to form meaningful relationships is degraded by the constant mistrust.

Social isolation and alienation

People who develop the social isolation schema develop the belief that they are different from everyone else. This can be for positive reasons, such as because they are smarter than everyone else, or for negative reasons, such as they are worth less than everyone else. Because of this belief, they begin to think that they cannot ever fit in or identify with others, or that they should not associate with others due to their uniqueness. Because they are so different, they believe there are no other people they can really connect with, even though in reality, someone else has likely had similar experiences, interests, and thoughts. This makes it difficult for them to find friends because they are constantly inundated with people they feel cannot relate to them. Oftentimes, for narcissists, this schema either feeds into their delusions of grandeur or their feeling of worthlessness. Their inability to connect with others is seen as either proof that they are unique and more important or as proof of their worthlessness.

Emotional Deprivation

People with this schema have come to believe that they will never find someone else that will give them the emotional attention and care they need to feel supported. They constantly feel deprived of support they need, and because of this, they find that they have a hard time leaning on others. They constantly expect to be denied or let down, so they oftentimes stop trying. By no longer really trying to seek out that emotional support they crave, however, they only solidify that thought in their mind as they continue to be unsupported due to not letting anyone know they need it. This self-affirming cycle perpetuates itself indefinitely until someone or something snaps them out of it.

Defectiveness and shame

When falling victim to the defectiveness and shame schema, the person believes that she is defective in some way. Whether physically unattractive or incapable of meeting a certain goal, emotionally needy or unstable, or less intelligent than those around him, these people always find faults with themselves. Oftentimes, they believe that their defects or shortcomings make them undesirable as friends or romantic partners, and their undesirability makes them unworthy of love from others. They become ashamed of their assumed shortcomings or perceived defects and struggle to believe that anyone could possibly care for them as their true selves, using this as further justification for needing to present themselves as their personas.

Impaired Limits

Entitlement and Grandiosity

This schema involves the person to feel that they are worth more than those around him. This is one of the key features of the narcissist, as he believes he is automatically more important than everyone else for no reason other than he is. These people feel like they deserve better treatment and privileges than everyone around them and that everyone should automatically recognize and respect his natural authority. These people oftentimes seek to control others and seek fame and power, even if it has to come at the expense of the needs of others. Ultimately, to this person, only his needs are important because of his superior status, and he will have no qualms with letting other people's needs go unmet if that means that his every whim has been satisfied.

Poor self-discipline

This schema causes individuals to lack tolerance for discomfort or setbacks. Due to not being able to handle setbacks or difficult situations, they instead give up to save themselves the trouble. The success is not worth the effort for these people, and they fail simply by not bothering to complete the work in the first place. Likewise, these people often struggle with controlling impulses or outbursts when emotions are high, causing issues with staying on task or when handling a difficult situation. Their emotions become overwhelming, and they end up failing due to their lack of discipline or ability to control themselves.

Impaired Autonomy and performance
Failure

People with this particular schema have a strong belief that they have never managed to succeed. Even past successes are seen as failures, with some sort of flaw being the reason it was a failure. For example, not getting a perfect score on a test may be deemed a failure because questions were missed. Because of their belief, they have always failed in the past; these people often feel as if they will always fail in the future as well, regardless of what the task is. Even something that they are good at or have done well at in the past will be seen as an impossibility.

Vulnerability to harm

This schema convinces people that they are at a higher risk of injury or illness. Even though there may be no basis for this thought, they constantly fear to get hurt or sick. This leads to fear and distrust, constantly thinking that those around are out to hurt the person with this schema, and the constant fear of getting hurt or ill may hold the person back from normal living. For example, if someone fears getting hurt, they may choose to avoid driving or walking along busy roads out of fear of being hit by a car. Someone who is sick may avoid crowds or doctors' offices when they need to see a doctor out of fear of contracting a serious illness in the waiting room.

Enmeshment

People with an enmeshment schema feel as if they cannot live without support from a specific person. They usually latch onto a major relationship in their lives, such as with a spouse or parent, and feel incapable without constant support. They develop a serious dependency on the other person, whether it is as an emotional crutch or to get them out of trouble when they are struggling, and have a strong aversion to being away from whoever they have attached to. Without the presence of the chosen person, they feel empty and incomplete, and they often become increasingly more demanding on the person's time and energy.

Dependence and incompetence

People falling victim to this schema feel incapable and incompetent. They feel as if they are unable to do anything on their own, and feel reliant on significant amounts of assistance from others. They may be unable to work without the support off the other person, whether through driving the person to and from work, or feel as if they cannot stay on task on their own. They find themselves afraid to try without someone else's support, and their reservations keep them from flourishing or proving themselves wrong and showing that they can actually be independent and competent if they try and apply themselves. They may even unconsciously sabotage their own attempts, believing they are unable to succeed on their own.

Overvigilance or Inhibition

Emotional inhibition

This schema gets people stopping or censoring themselves in fear of other people's reactions. They essentially force themselves to bottle up all of their thoughts and feelings rather than potentially inconveniencing someone else. They put themselves last and hide their true feelings in hopes of keeping the people around them satisfied. Oftentimes, these people will go along with anything, even if it means doing something they hate because they would rather suffer in silence than lose a relationship with someone they deem important.

Unrelenting standards

When people have unrelenting standards, they often set goals that are excessive or unattainable, even though failing will cause damage to their lives. They constantly set impossible expectations and try to meet them, even when a reasonable person may recognize that they are impossible. They also frequently aim for perfection and believe anything short of that perfection they aspire to achieve is a failure. This black-and-white thinking leaves them in a constant state of failure as they fail to meet their impossible, unreasonable standards.

Negativity and pessimism

This schema paints the world grey and has the people with this mindset, only seeing the bad parts of life. They focus in on the negative, such as sad or difficult times, and ignore the positive aspects. While they may have had a perfectly good day, they may define the day as bad due to one small incident, such as spilling a drink or getting the wrong order at lunch. The tiniest inconvenience could be enough for a person stuck in a negativity schema to say the entire day was horrible, even if she had spent the day at an amusement park with her loved ones, doing everything she wanted. She would focus instead on the fact that she got a sunburn, spent too much time waiting in line for one ride, and that time she got splashed by a water ride was horrible. They always find something to complain about and never acknowledge the good parts.

Punitiveness

People that fall into the habit of the punitiveness schema believe that any error, no matter how serious or harmless, deserves to be criticized and punished. They are often just as harsh on themselves as others, and are quick to angrily correct people around them that misstep or make a mistake, even if it was a harmless misunderstanding.

These people fail to acknowledge that we all make mistakes at some point in life, and also refuse to consider that sometimes, circumstances could reasonably explain the error as a mistake that anyone would make as opposed to it being from negligence or incompetence.

Other-directedness

Self-sacrifice

This schema makes people willingly forego their needs so they can ensure that someone else's are met. They frequently feel guilty about their own needs or wants, and worry that if they fail to make sure the other person is cared for, that the other person will be unable to meet those needs or will suffer somehow. While some level of putting other people's needs first is normal in certain contexts, such as a mother making sure her children are fed and cared for before herself, selflessness to the extent that your own needs are met is dysfunctional and can be harmful. These people neglect themselves to care for others, and this sacrifice only hurts themselves.

Approval seeking

People with the approval seeking schema require validation from others. They will seek it out relentlessly, and try to do things they think will gain appreciation from others, such as buying their friends drinks, or agreeing to go to a restaurant they hate or a to a concert they have no interest in. These people focus so much on getting approval from other people that they never get a chance to develop a healthy sense of self-worth. Their entire existence and value become dependent on other people's opinions; this leaves them constantly seeking to please those around them, regardless of the cost to themselves.

Subjugation

People who find themselves stuck in the subjugation schema feel as if they are pressured or forced into giving up their needs or wants by other people. They believe that these other people will threaten them if they refuse to comply. These threats can be anything from physical harm to withholding affection or attention. This keeps the people with the schema stuck feeling as if they have to give up their needs willingly or they will be taken anyway.

Testing Schemas

During the course of treating maladaptive schemas, rules for each schema are defined. Each schema has rules that keep the schema valid and prove it true. This works because they help the individual with the schema avoid catastrophic or triggering situations related to the schema. An example of this is someone with the self-sacrifice schema saying that he should never take care of himself because in taking care of himself, he is selfishly ignoring the needs of his loved ones and letting them down. In order to not feel as if he is selfish, he then makes it a point to avoid selfishly meeting his own needs. He dutifully puts his needs last and makes sure those around him are happy, even though this may be at a detriment to him. This is because he cannot cope with the guilt that comes with putting himself first. Since he feels like he cannot cope, he instead creates a rule of never putting himself first to ensure that he never ends up feeling intense guilt in the first place.

Once these rules are identified, they must be tested or challenged. Often, this is done with the therapist's guidance in a controlled situation, so they are able to slowly realize that their rules were flawed from the beginning. These rules are tested systematically with three main steps. First, the person needs to pick a situation related to the schema that will cause a small amount of fear or discomfort. They then plan out a reaction that will contradict the schema's rules. This reaction is healthier and productive, and the fact that it contradicts the schema's rules makes it a valid way to begin to disprove the schema. Lastly, the person needs to identify whether the predicted catastrophe or triggering event happened, and if the catastrophe was avoided, he must record what actually happened instead.

For example, a man with an abandonment schema may frequently find himself skirting around issues with his girlfriend, avoiding any heavy discussions and always deferring to her on any serious decisions. He fears that telling her his true opinions will make her think less of him, and once she thinks less of him, she will abandon him and find someone she deems more compatible or better than him. Once this abandonment schema is identified, he will then be asked to imagine a situation where he tells her his true thoughts. He may decide on telling her what he wants for dinner that night when she suggests dinner at the Thai restaurant he hates for their weekly date night. Then, with the help of his therapist, he role-plays how the conversation would go. He tells her nicely that he does not like Thai food, and really only went for her in the past. He imagines her laughing it off and telling him to be honest with her in the future, so he is not miserable. He identifies that the catastrophe he imagined, her abandoning him for having bad taste or disagreeing with her, did not occur, and feels a little more comfortable truly confronting her in person rather than role-playing it. Over time, with real-life experience, the schema's rule is slowly contradicted and loses power, and the test reveals that the schema's rule was false.

As the schema is disproved, it is important to begin establishing healthier thoughts as well. The man with an abandonment schema may tell himself that his loved ones will accept him for who he is, even if they have some disagreements between the two of them, or if they have conflicting interests. He will then begin creating healthier rules that affirm his belief in himself, with his daily interactions with those around him affirming it. As people do not decide they hate him for having his own taste in food, style, or music, he begins to discover that the people who really value him will stick around, even if they disagree with his taste.

Coping

Coping with these schemas can be incredibly testing when you are on the receiving end of the behaviors. It is important to remember that these schemas are coping mechanisms in their own rights. Even though you may see them as unhealthy or disordered, it is important to recognize them for what they are. They are the results of a person who has been broken down or neglected, attempting to manage overwhelming feelings of insecurity. They are not necessarily meant to hurt those around the narcissist.

By remembering that the narcissist is doing the best he can to navigate through the world with a broken sense of self and lacking healthy coping mechanisms, it may be easier to accept the behavior. Just as you would not be offended when a child throws a temper tantrum over not going her way because she has not learned better yet, it may help to remember that the narcissist also lacks these fundamental skills. Skills that you may take for granted, such as being able to cope with disappointment or conflict, are actually the result of years of experiences and guidance through difficult situations when you were younger. Through understanding what may motivate the narcissist to behave the way he does, it becomes easier to react productively to the behaviors.

CHAPTER 7

The Narcissist's Awareness

Narcissists are notoriously stubborn and difficult to get through to. Their lack of empathy and grandiose behaviors can make it hard for them to really understand the wider impact of their behaviors beyond just getting what they want when they want it. Sometimes, through raising the narcissist's awareness of what she is doing and how it is causing problems, you can begin to improve their behaviors. Rarely, they will be willing to improve themselves, especially if they are relatively low in narcissistic traits, or they are borderline narcissistic but do not have a diagnosis. Those who are more narcissistic by nature will likely be much more disagreeable about the process and less willing to even entertain the idea that they are not perfect exactly the way they are. Remember, narcissists typically lack normal self-awareness and see the world through a distorted lens. It will take plenty of patience to raise the narcissist's awareness, and if you feel like it is too much for you, there is no shame in saying you cannot handle it.

Willing Interactions

For those few narcissists who are willing to improve themselves or recognize their shortcomings, discussions of problematic behavior can be quite useful. Just as you would take a child aside to discuss why it is not okay to behave a certain way, you can also tactfully discuss why something the narcissist is doing is more hurtful. Remember, narcissists have fragile egos, so tact is of the utmost importance.

For example, if the narcissist has a tendency to seek perfection and you suspect a schema of unrelenting standards, you may look for ways that you notice the narcissist succeeding and comment on them. When you notice the narcissist begin to nitpick at himself or other people, pointing out flaws, it could be acceptable to gently remind the narcissist that small flaws will not be a problem. Point out that perfection, while a fantastic concept, is rarely ever a goal that is productive, and comment on how you have noticed how harsh he is on himself and others. Identify that no one is really comfortable with the insistence of flawless and that his expectations make it difficult to work. By identifying the problem you and your coworkers may have, you have provided some awareness to the narcissist, so he recognizes that part of his behavior is problematic. By providing him with praise, you may challenge one of his schema's rules. This sort of conversations repeated over time can be beneficial to the narcissist, and may even ultimately challenge the schema enough for him to relent, even if only a little.

By pointing out his unwarranted harshness toward himself, you begin to plant the seed of the idea that perfection is not necessary. He may have developed these unrelenting standards due to a childhood of strict adherence to perfection and could have been punished unfairly when they were not met. It is important to remember to treat the narcissist with the same grace you would use for a child still learning how to interact with the world. Do not feel discouraged or irritated if you have to continue to gently guide the narcissist toward the idea that less than perfect can still be successful.

It can also be useful to discuss with the narcissist that his actions can make him come across as harsh, or make people prefer to avoid him. This hangs another carrot in front of the narcissist: Attention. Narcissists crave positive attention and admiration, so the idea that being a little less unrelenting may bring more of that attention could be a fantastic motivator.

Unknowing Interactions

More often than not, the narcissist is not open to consciously correcting her behavior. True to her diagnosis, she is unwilling or unable to acknowledge that she may be any sort of a problem. If you were to approach her and say that something she is doing is a problem, she would likely explode at you, unleashing her narcissistic rage at you because you have just become a challenge to her distorted worldview. It is easier to chase you away than to accept that her view is flawed. With these people, much more tact is necessary.

Much like how you noticed the narcissist's unrelenting standards in the previous section, you should also look for the unwilling narcissist's schemas. Perhaps she has a tendency to distrust others, and because of that distrust, she is quick to accuse others around her as the problem and constantly sabotaging relationships because she would rather be alone than vulnerable to others. This makes her especially difficult to work with, and you often find yourself unhappy when work requires you to interact with her.

Rather than accepting the narcissist's haughty attitude, you can use her distrustful nature to your advantage; always follow through with what you offer to do, even if it is met with ungratefulness. If you offer to bring her a coffee, follow through with it, even if she accuses you of doing it to get her to do more of the work. She is distrustful of you because you have not given her a reason to trust you. If you offer to go over her paperwork to check for errors before submitting a group project for work, do it and make sure to sandwich any criticism between praises of things that are working well in the project. This not only lessens the blow to her ego but makes her feel less like you are intentionally trying to hurt her when you have more compliments than criticisms.

No matter what, you need to avoid affirming her rule of avoiding trusting people. Even when it is difficult, it is imperative that you try your hardest to follow through with everything you say you will do. Even if you have been making good progress, a single slip up could send all of that progress down the drain.

Over time, through plenty of diligence and working with the narcissist's traits instead of being offended and affirming the maladaptive schemas, you will begin to tear the schemas down. Eventually, she may recognize that you are not out to get her and are genuinely trying to help. When the narcissist is unwilling to admit fault, it is important to let the narcissist arrive at that conclusion without you saying it, making it their decision rather than them feeling as if they are bowing down to someone else.

Care and Practice

Ultimately, when trying to raise a narcissist's awareness of his disordered behavior, you must learn their schemas to the best of your ability and take special care to control the triggers that make the narcissist feel a need to act upon their schemas. Their schemas are poor attempts at coping with stress and discomfort, and remembering that can help you remember to have the compassion and understanding that the narcissist is not necessarily trying to hurt you, but is acting true to his nature. Understanding the narcissist's core self and recognizing it as his attempt to control the world to protect himself can help you remember that it is important to avoid known triggers if it is practical or reasonable. Think of this as knowing not to poke the sleeping bear, no matter how tempting it may be.

While you should never goad the narcissist into known behaviors by using their known triggers, you should also never force yourself to walk on eggshells around him. If the only reasonable answer to a situation is something that may trigger the narcissist, then that is understandable. Do your best to control the triggers, but do not dedicate your life to constantly placating the narcissist, as this will only feed into his sense of entitlement.

While taking care to avoid triggers when possible, you should also practice techniques that help establish a healthy relationship and create positive interactions between yourself and the narcissist. As discussed earlier, remember that working with the narcissist's schemas can help you begin to develop a more meaningful relationship built upon trust that you will not hurt them the way they have been hurt in the past. He may begin to recognize that you are there as support rather than as another adversary wanting to tear him down, and you may find his behaviors becoming healthier and more productive as he has less and less reason to use his maladaptive schemas to cope with stress.

CHAPTER 8

Maintaining Yourself

When dealing with a narcissist, you find yourself having to make plenty of concessions to avoid meltdowns or outrages. With narcissists, you often feel as if you have to make a choice between pleasing yourself or the narcissist, and it's frequently easier to forego what you want than it is to deal with the backlash from the narcissist. It is important to make sure you maintain your own sense of self during the process of dealing with a narcissist, and you need to be able to understand what the appropriate steps are to maintaining yourself. You need to

Maintaining Yourself

know when flexibility is useful or if setting boundaries will be a better course of action. You also need to understand when enough is enough so you can take a step back from the situation and disengage from the narcissist for your own physical and emotional safety. Learning these skills will give you a much better grasp of how to interact with a narcissist while minimizing damage for everyone involved.

Bending, Not Breaking

Just as the tree bends to the wind to keep from breaking, sometimes being flexible with your own expectations is the best choice when it comes to dealing with a narcissist. Narcissists are stubborn by nature; they want everything to go their way and struggle to cope when things do not play out as they expect. The average person is much better at coping with small missteps in their plans without being tripped up, and sometimes, the easiest way to maintain yourself and your sanity is to remain flexible. If the concession is something you truly do not care about, it is likely not worth the battle of remaining firm. Pick your battles and let the narcissist have her way if you are indifferent.

Your own self-awareness and self-restraint will be two of your greatest defenses against falling victim to narcissistic behaviors. Unlike the narcissist, you can recognize when you are wrong without sending your world shattering around you, and you can also restrain yourself when something does go wrong. You have developed proper coping mechanisms and have learned to handle stress in healthy, productive ways that do not worsen your problems. Remembering to utilize your self-awareness will keep you aware that you are angry or frustrated with the narcissist. This recognition allows you to be aware that you may be more prone to lashing out at the narcissist at that moment, which also allows you to utilize your self-restraint. You can remind yourself to stop, take a deep breath, and count to four before reacting to keep from impulsively lashing out.

For example, imagine your husband is a narcissist: He is very resistant to change in plans and finds himself unable to cope with the stress that comes with the unexpected. Perhaps you two had been planning a two-day trip, in which one day you go see a play you were kind of interested in seeing, and the next day you go to an event your husband is excited to go to. When you arrive at your trip destination, you realize that the play and the event your husband really wanted to go to overlap and notice that you had written the date wrong when you were planning. Despite some mild disappointment, you realize

Maintaining Yourself

that you are still mostly indifferent about the play in the first place. Instead of insisting on going, you tell your husband that you will skip it and the two of you will go to his event instead, so you do not miss it. This means your husband is not facing a change in schedule that will leave him stressed and possibly trigger a negative behavior, and the two of you still go on to enjoy your trip. Ultimately, your self-awareness allows you to recognize that you had only planned on going because there was nothing else interesting enough during that time, and you had little interest in it beyond filling the empty time. Your flexibility kept your vacation lighthearted, and your husband remained happy. This is an example of an appropriate time to be flexible.

Remember, by remaining flexible when applicable, you keep yourself from breaking. Your flexibility keeps you strong and able to withstand the difficult behaviors that come from the narcissist. Your patience will keep you firm as you encounter the same issues over and over, and your self-awareness will help you acknowledge your feelings so you can cope with them in a healthy, productive way.

Setting Boundaries

Now, if the play was actually something you were really interested in, and you realized that there would be a second day your husband's event was happening that would not conflict with the play's actual date, you would require less flexibility. In this case, you would be better off setting a boundary. You have strong feelings about something, and you should not have to give in to the narcissist's demands just because he struggles to cope sometimes.

Setting boundaries involves you standing firm on an issue. This can be anything you feel strongly about. Oftentimes, boundaries involve respect and an expectation to be treated with basic human decency. People want to live without being harassed or hurt, and they expect to be given that opportunity. When they fight to get that treatment, they have set a boundary that they will not tolerate being crossed. Oftentimes, there is some sort of consequence for crossing the boundary, such as damaging the friendship or causing the wronged party to take a step back and disengage from the relationship altogether.

Even though some flexibility is necessary when dealing with a narcissist, setting boundaries is still important as well. You must be able to balance when flexibility is important, and when it is something that you must be firm on. Oftentimes, these boundaries need to be set if it will cause you physical or emotional harm. A reasonable boundary is telling your narcissistic spouse to respect your decision on something you feel strongly about without lashing out when he disagrees. Being firm that you are entitled to your own opinion, even if he does not like it, is normal and healthy. Telling him that you insist on going to the play you really want to see because you and he can go to his event the next day as well is reasonable. It is also reasonable for you to tell him that you will not accept him angrily lashing out at you when plans change.

When you do set a boundary with a narcissist, it is important that you follow through with whatever consequence you have set. If you tell your narcissistic husband that you will disengage from the conversation altogether if he cannot use respectful language or a respectful tone with you, you need to do so if he continues to say cruel things. If you do not follow through with enforcing your boundary, you are telling the narcissist that they are negotiable and that in the right situations at the right time, those boundaries can be crossed with no consequence. This gives the narcissist what he wants without working on getting it, and teaches the narcissist that his techniques work. He will continue to use name-calling and belittling to get his way, and you will have less of a standing to demand what you want after you have given in.

Think of the narcissist's reaction to your boundaries as a temper tantrum. You would not give in to a toddler's demands for a cookie at bedtime just because he is pouting, screaming, crying, and hitting because you would teach him that pouting, screaming, crying, and hitting is a valid way to get what he wants. Any time someone tells him no, he will scream and cry, fully expecting to get what he wants because it worked with the cookie. The narcissist will learn in the same way, so it is easier to remain firm, even if you ultimately decide after the fact that it is not as important to you as you initially thought. By keeping these boundaries firm and enforcing consequences when they are ignored, you protect yourself from much of the narcissistic abuse that is common in relationships or friendships with narcissists.

Drawing Lines in the Sand

Sometimes, despite your best efforts, a relationship becomes toxic and unbearable. No matter how hard you try or what you do, the narcissist continuously hurts you emotionally, and you are feeling less and less like yourself. In these cases, it is time to draw a line in the

Maintaining Yourself

sand and walk away. Walking away is not the easy way out, despite what those around you might say; it will require immense self-discipline and willpower to walk away from someone you may deeply love, and it is okay to do so when you are being hurt.

Abuse is always a reason to end a relationship, even if it is caused by a mental illness or disorder. While you may have sworn in sickness and in health in wedding vows, that did not include a risk to your own health. You must take care of yourself before you are able to help anyone else, and if you feel as if you are being abused or mistreated, leaving is totally acceptable. Think of this as the ultimate boundary: You expect to not be on the receiving end of intentional harm, physical or emotional, from the other person. When that person intentionally harms you, that line has been irrevocably crossed, and the thought of the other person doing that again will always loom in the background, coloring your relationship. You do not have to live like that. You are entitled to live a life free of pain, and with respect every person deserves.

Even when a relationship does not involve physically harming you, sometimes the emotional toll it takes is too much. You find yourself constantly drained and like you can no longer enjoy the things that used to bring you pleasure. People may be telling you that you seem depressed, but in reality, you are drained by a relationship. Perhaps your parent is always downplaying every achievement you have, to the point that you believe that you are worthless and incapable of success. Maybe your best friend is constantly one-upping you, so you feel like you are wrong to feel proud of whatever accomplishments you achieve because she is always better. It could be a coworker who belittles and berates you every time you make a mistake, no matter how small.

Regardless of what the nature of the relationship is, taking a step back and cutting the narcissist off is almost always an option. When an entire cut-off is not possible due to sharing minor children, or because you live in such close proximity to the other person, you can take a huge step back and keep the relationship and interactions with the person as minimal as possible to avoid further exposure to their toxicity. It may not be easy, but just as you would not willingly spend time around a rattlesnake just because you have plenty of antivenin readily available, you should not spend time around toxic people. Their toxicity will eat away at you as time goes by, rendering you a husk of your former self.

Maintaining Yourself

After cutting off or limiting contact with the narcissist, you will begin to feel more like your old self, and you may realize just how much of a toll that relationship had taken. In hindsight, you may suddenly see all of the red flags and wonder how you managed to get yourself ensnared in such a big mess in the first place. Remember, narcissists, are typically masters at manipulating people around them, feeling it is necessary to their survival and mental health to do so. You are not the first, and you will not be the last, person to get ensnared in a toxic narcissist's web of lies, and you should not beat yourself up over it after deciding to break free.

CHAPTER 9

Different Contexts

While narcissists typically share similar traits with one another, challenges and conflicts with a narcissist can vary greatly based on the type of relationship you have with him. A workplace relationship with a narcissist often looks vastly different than a familial or romantic relationship with a narcissist, which will be different from a platonic friendship with a narcissist. Understanding how these different relationships present will help you to identify when you are interacting with a narcissist as opposed to someone who is just naturally abrasive or withdrawn. Of course, understanding when you are interacting with a narcissist will help you know how to interact with that particular person.

Workplace

Workplace relationships with narcissists can be particularly difficult. You go into work expecting a degree of professionalism but are met instead with the narcissist. They are scathing, desire perfection at all times, and are not above demeaning or belittling those who never meet their unrealistic, impossible standards. Oftentimes, a narcissistic boss will claim credit for anything her team produces, as the team is seen as little more than an extension of the boss, and therefore their work is her work by default. She will favor certain people that are useful for her, and those who are not are typically ignored when they are not being hassled about something.

Expect your narcissistic boss or coworker to be completely insensitive and blind to your needs. Unless you are providing her with premium work and are turning it in, she does not want to deal with you. Problems will be ignored or brushed off, and you will be used as little more than a tool to keep her well-oiled machine running perfectly. You are expected to play that role without complaint.

Keeping in mind that narcissists have sensitive egos, you should use tact whenever you have to interact. Pointing out mistakes or contradicting the narcissist typically only causes more trouble than it solves, and if you dare injure her ego, she will likely explode on you. She will either deny any blame, redirecting it onto other people, or she will lash out at others. Remembering the narcissist's penchant for perfection and lack of ability to cope with criticism, you would be best advised to avoid angering the narcissist and sticking to getting your work done whenever possible if the narcissist is not abusive or toxic.

Platonic

People often don't think narcissists are capable of friendships, and while narcissists do lack an ability to create healthy relationships, some do seek to make friendships. Often, these friendships are developed because you have something that the narcissist admires or envies, and she has gravitated toward you to either learn to emulate you or to get access to what she wanted.

In the beginning, she will do what she can to impress you to gain your attention. She will claim to share hobbies with you, even if she knows next to nothing about whatever interest you have. She will agree with you constantly and maybe make comments about how you two

Different Contexts

are so compatible. She shows you the best side of her, and once she is convinced that your friendship is securely developed, she begins to aim for what she wants. If she wants someone to compare herself to in order to make herself feel better, she may poke at anything you are self-conscious about to remind you that ultimately, she is superior. She also may suddenly have emergencies any time you needed her help, using this excuse to avoid doing anything remotely supportive for you. You may think nothing of it until you notice the pattern of her never being available.

Even worse, sometimes, she demands to be the center of attention. She will aim to one-up the guest of honor at a celebration. If you are having a baby shower, she may announce that she is pregnant as well, with twins, while you are opening presents. At your wedding reception, she may announce she is engaged during her speech. If you get a new-to-you car, she will suddenly have the same one, but in the newest model with a higher trim. She seeks to better you in every situation, possible with no regard for how this makes you feel.

Ultimately, you end up stuck, deciding between ending the friendship or continuing to accept her behaviors. She will likely never be reliable for emotional support and will likely always try to be better than you in all situations. Oftentimes, however, she makes the decision for you, and as soon as she gets bored, she will vanish from your life as quickly as she had appeared.

If you do wish to salvage the friendship, it can be useful for you to remind yourself what about your friend interested you in the first place. By keeping your focus on the positive aspects your friend brings to your life, you may find yourself slowly becoming more accepting of her shortcomings as you recognize them as a part of her as opposed to an intentional dig at you. Keeping your friend's narcissistic personality in mind and recognizing that she will always have those tendencies can help remind you to remain patient, while also reminding you to keep your expectations for her realistic and reasonable. Do not expect her to be emotionally supportive when you know that is something she cannot easily provide, as that would only set her up for failure. Instead, focus on what you enjoy about her and keep your interactions with her as positive as possible.

Romantic

Romantic relationships with narcissists often start out like fairytales. Everything seems perfect, and the narcissist is exactly your type. He displays all the traits you find

Different Contexts

especially attractive, such as being an attentive listener, intelligent, or interested in the same obscure sub-genre of movies as you. You feel as if you two have so much in common, and think it must be fate. Love, at first sight, is often used to describe these interactions.

However, his attentiveness is frequently more manipulative than kind; he uses it to learn all about how your mind works. He will learn what makes you feel loved and what your insecurities are. At first, he will use this insight to make you feel loved. His goal is to make you as attached to him as possible in as short of a period of time as possible, knowing that the relationship will not work if he shows his true self before you have fallen in love. He does not want to show his manipulative side to you until he knows you will not leave him at his first major transgression.

He will push for the relationship to progress quicker than normal, always wanting more. He wants to spend more and more time with you, asking you to go on dates more. He seeks to consume your valuable time, edging out competition from friends or family. You are quickly becoming his primary source of narcissistic supply, and he wants to make sure he has you all to himself. He may ask you to marry him or move in with him far sooner than is reasonable to most people, and as soon as he feels like you are well attached, he drops his act. He becomes demeaning and cruel, using all of the insecurities he has learned to manipulate you and keep you subdued and complacent. Over time, this behavior escalates, slowly acclimating you to the narcissist's true self. You find yourself soon accepting behaviors that would have been immediate deal-breakers during the first stages of a relationship.

Co-parent

Sometimes, you find yourself in the situation of having children with a narcissist, but you have chosen to end any romantic relationship with him. Co-parenting is difficult on its own, but adding in a narcissist to the equation is asking for trouble. Because you and the narcissist share children, you are likely legally obligated to foster some semblance of a relationship between the narcissist and his children. No matter how much you may wish to completely cut off contact, you will be required to maintain some level of contact for your children's best interest.

Narcissists typically struggle to parent. Lacking empathy, they struggle to really understand their children's emotional needs. They may make sure the child's physical

Different Contexts

needs are met but do not nurture their children. Despite knowing this, if you have a court order, you are required to offer your children to their other parent. You should be prepared for your narcissistic ex to manipulate the children in order to get back at you or use them as a way to get a response when you are ignoring him. He will be quick to utilize his own rights to the children when it is an inconvenience for you, but when it is inconvenient for him, he will not bother exercising his time with the children.

Ultimately, what he wants is control over your life, and being in control of a portion of his children's time gives him this over you by default. He knows that a good parent will not leave their children stranded or home alone, so he may call in the middle of the night to have you come and get them, especially if he knows it will interfere with other plans you had. He will lie to your children about why they cannot do things they want, returning the blame to you in hopes of hurting you by ruining your relationship with your child. He will call incessantly during times people are typically unavailable, such as during dinner or during your children's extracurricular activities, and if you dare suggest that the children are unavailable, he will say you are alienating the children and impeding on his relationship with them.

Ultimately, when co-parenting with a narcissist, you have to recognize that the narcissist does not have his children's best interest at heart. He will do things that work for him, even if it is harmful to the shared children, and he will not think twice about hurting them emotionally. He may draw the line at physically abusing them, but his emotional unavailability and lack of nurturing is still a form of emotional abuse.

Children Exhibiting Narcissistic Traits and Charges

With both children and adult charges, you are in control of everything. You control the environment, the scheduling, exposure to media and people, and just about every other aspect of life. This puts you in a great position to begin alleviating narcissistic tendencies or behaviors. Dealing with both children and charges have a lot of similarities: You influence their behaviors by influencing and controlling the environment and potential triggers for maladaptive behavior. They also differ greatly in that children are children while charges could be adults. However, despite the age difference, the advice for handling children often also carries over to adult charges, though the execution should be altered to reflect the proper audience.

Different Contexts

It is important to note that children are not yet old enough to be diagnosed as narcissists, but they do often exhibit narcissistic traits. Narcissists never developed proper coping methods for stress, so it should be no surprise that children often behave similarly to narcissists. The good news is that children often outgrow these behaviors, though that does not mean you should not try to correct them.

One of the upsides of having minor children with narcissistic traits is that you can control their environment with hopes of influencing their behaviors while their minds are still developing. You can begin your intervention early before it evolves into a full-blown narcissistic personality disorder, and hopefully, teach your children to develop a healthy sense of self and proper coping methods. With adult charges, you have missed the window for shaping the developing brain, but you can still influence patterns of thinking and seek to begin testing and disproving plenty of the charge's maladaptive schemas.

Since you now understand that narcissistic personality disorder often consists of a lack of a healthy sense of self, low self-esteem, and a lack of empathy, you should be able to see those as areas your child needs extra support in developing, or that your charge needs help in learning. Create situations that encourage and reward your child, while fostering a sense of empathy for those around him. For your charges, make sure you create interactions that allow you to model empathy so they can begin to learn how to interact with a healthy level of empathizing with others. You can also make it a point to empathize with the narcissistic charge, verbally discussing it in the most tactful way possible. For example, saying to your angry charge, "Wow, I can see that you are really angry right now. I would be too if I were losing the game. You look like you need some time to cool off. Come over when you calm down, and we can continue this game then." Keep it calm, direct, and do not back down from requiring the narcissist to be calm before continuing. You have acknowledged his feelings, validated them, provided a getaway from the stressful situation, and created an incentive for the narcissist to calm down rather than blow up.

You can cultivate empathy by empathizing with your child and modeling empathy for others. While it may seem childish, you can talk through this process as you do it, so your child really gets the idea. For example, if your child has been disappointed and is crying while teetering toward throwing a temper tantrum, you should stop, get down on your child's level, and place a hand on his shoulder. Tell him that it is okay to be disappointed, and it is okay to cry, but a tantrum and not listening is unacceptable. Get him to take a few deep breaths to calm down, and ask if he wants a hug. By identifying and validating his feelings before giving him a technique to cope with them, he feels acknowledged and may begin to follow your instructions and calm down, especially if you tell him about a time you were disappointed and sad once too. You can further model empathy by empathizing for others. Imagine that you are at the store with your child, and you see a busy mother with two young children in the cart. She accidentally drops her eggs, shattering them and making a mess all over the tile. You can tell your child that that is too bad; she looks sad and overwhelmed. Then ask him what you should do to help. If he does not come to the conclusion of helping her clean the mess, or seeking out an employee to get help, you can suggest doing so to the child. If age appropriate, allow him to go through the effort of helping, and praise him when he has finished. Remind him that he helped her during a tough time, that it was a very nice thing to do, and then ask him if he feels good after being such a big helper to someone in need. Try not to buy him a treat or reward at the store, as he may associate doing good deeds as being done solely for rewards.

In order to cultivate self-esteem, remember to never be critical of your child or your charge. It is good to correct behavior, but there is a fine line between productive corrections and harsh criticisms. Knowing to toe the line will help you avoid accidentally crushing any developing self-esteem, your child or charge may have. Remember to praise your child or charge's successes when appropriate and give him plenty of opportunities to succeed at tasks. Rather than seeing this as coddling or babying, think of it as no different than him spraining an ankle and needing a crutch. The crutch is necessary to help keep weight off of the ankle so it can heal, and your praise and avoidance of criticism will help your child or charge to develop a healthy self-esteem that will carry him far.

SECTION 3

Working with Others outside the Circle

CHAPTER 10

Family and Triggers

When we are stressed, afraid, or in need of support, one of the first sources we often turn to is family. These people have supported us in our lives up until this point, and we often see our family, especially those older than us, as a valuable source of sage advice and wisdom. However, when dealing with a narcissist or narcissistic abuse, family may not really understand. They may not understand what you are going through and may not even know what narcissistic personality disorder is. Though they mean well, you will have to educate them, strategically teaching them about the disorder in a way that will help them support you in the way you need. Do not be afraid to tell them exactly what you need for them, or even to hand over a copy of this book to read in order to help them understand what you are going through. Family typically will go out of their way to help family members in need, if they know their help is needed. Just as you likely would not hesitate if a family member turned to you for support, many members of your family will also gladly help you if you reach out.

Mental Health

Mental health is something that many people are ignorant of. As our mental state is largely invisible to those around us, it is something that many do not understand. You need to be prepared to have a discussion about this with your family if they prove to be ignorant of the seriousness of mental health issues. You should be able to discuss that mental health is just as important as physical health and that it is not always as easy to recognize a mental health issue as opposed to a personality flaw. Especially if they know the narcissist, they likely see the narcissist as successful, confident, and essentially perfect, only seeing his mask as opposed to who he really is.

Family and Triggers

You should gently breach the subject, mentioning that while you love your narcissistic partner, the behaviors are beginning to wear down on you. Emphasize that the narcissist is not necessarily trying to hurt you, but his personality disorder is making your relationship increasingly more difficult. It may feel strange to be on the lecturing side of the relationship, especially if you are primarily speaking with parents or grandparents. They also may struggle to take what you are saying as worth accepting if they are accustomed to being the ones in leadership positions. Ultimately, it will be up to you to help them navigate the muddy water that is understanding a narcissist, and showing them how to best support you during your journey.

Ultimately, you need to show your family that you are trying to protect or prioritize your own satisfaction in life. Life is far too short to waste tiptoeing around issues, and you are making an effort to either help the narcissist improve his behavior, or you are working toward cutting off the narcissist, both of which will improve your quality of life. You should be firm that this is what is best for you, and that you would like their support in that matter. They may react generally positively to this, telling you that they will support you however you need, or they may react negatively, accusing him of hiding behind a pretend disorder to get away with unacceptable behavior.

It is important for you to remind your family that stigmatizing the narcissist's personality disorder is unproductive or counterproductive. Just as you would not shame someone for being ill or developing cancer, you should not shame those who struggle with mental illness. Remind your family that only a trained medical professional can really diagnose the behaviors and that they should not use a personality disorder to begin patronizing or belittling the narcissist.

Antagonizers in the Family

When members of your family insist on antagonizing you or the narcissist, offering none of the support you need, sometimes you need to reevaluate the relationship. Obviously, you do not want to spend time with people that will bring you down and make the already-difficult process of dealing with a narcissist even harder. When you find that you have family members that are particularly antagonistic, you may be better off making changes to how often you see them, if you choose to continue seeing them at all.

Family and Triggers

While family is important, and should absolutely be treated as such, the same rule applies here as does with narcissists: If the family is causing you pain or making your life unreasonably more stressful or difficult, it is acceptable to end the relationship, or even just put it on pause until you feel better equipped to deal with any negativity.

Think of support systems as large circles with rings inside. At the centermost ring is the person needing support, which is you in this case. Each ring that gets further away from the center is a degree further from the support. So, you are at the center, and your parents may be the second circle, as they are the closest to you. From there, your friends might be the third circle, and coworkers in the fourth, with everything outside of that circle being strangers or acquaintances. Support should only move inward. People in the second circle should only pour support to the person needing it, and they should only seek support from those further removed from the center of the circle. When people start pushing from support from or making things difficult for the inner circle, you begin to see a problem.

Luckily, there are multiple ways to limit the relationship with whoever is unsupportive of your journey through dealing with a narcissist. You can choose to avoid that person altogether, ending the relationship in its entirety. This keeps you from having to face the person at all during your stressful time. You can choose to take a step back from the relationship temporarily, which is essentially cutting off the person but only for a short period of time. This gives you time to cool off and get your thoughts straightened out while trying to deal with yourself. During this period, you will be focused on maintaining yourself, and you do not need any other adversaries to that sense of self while simultaneously dealing with a narcissist. You can also choose to moderately limit contact with this adversarial family, such as limiting interactions to amounts you can tolerate without feeling like it is detrimental to your wellbeing. You could choose to visit one day every month for dinner at a restaurant, rather than going to that person's house every weekend. This allows you to maintain a relationship with the people who are hindering you during your time trying to cope with a narcissist, while also taking enough of a step back that you no longer feel hindered.

Ultimately, any of these methods could aid in coping with unsupportive or antagonistic family members. It is up to you to decide how much exposure you want to their negativity or antagonism. It is reasonable for you to want to step back from a relationship, and being family is not a free pass to treat other family members poorly. If anything, you should hold your family members to higher standards than you would hold those around you, as you should expect those closest to you to treat you with more care and respect than perfect strangers do. Do not let family make your life difficult just because you share DNA. Family is not determined only by blood, and you are well within your rights to take a step back from people who are blood-related to you but only add strife to your life.

CHAPTER 11

Best Friends & Platonic Loves

While friends mean well and only want what is best for you, they may not be well informed, especially on the subject of mental health disorders, which are rarely well understood by those who have never had to deal with them. Your friends also may struggle to remain objective enough to understand that the narcissist likely does not mean to treat you the way he does. They may struggle to stay neutral enough to give you the support you need when they see you in pain, and they may struggle to not villainize the narcissist for behaving in such a way that causes you pain, whether it is intentional or not. They care about you enough that seeing you in pain can cloud their judgment.

Knowing that your friends may react in ways that they hope are beneficial, but do not help, informing them of what they can do is the best way to avoid disaster. While you do want your friends to understand your struggles, you do not want them doing something rash or detrimental to your attempts at dealing with a narcissist. For example, if you are working with a narcissistic spouse to get through therapy and try to better his behavior, you do not want to risk your friends saying something to the narcissist that immediately puts him on the defensive and leaves him lashing out in order to gain more control.

Just as with your family, you should be clear to your friends that this is a challenging endeavor, but one you want to attempt nonetheless. Despite the challenges, you want to remain committed to the narcissist, and you need their support as you work on how to do that. Tell your friends that you are trusting them to be there for you when you need them most, just as you would be there for them if they needed you, and the best way they can support you is by being there to listen to you when you need someone to talk to. Again, you may find it useful to recommend that your friends also look into what to expect with narcissists, and even sharing this book with them could provide valuable insight, so they learn how best to support someone suffering through a narcissistic relationship.

Triggering Friends

Ultimately, knowing that your friends may become upset, listening to your discussions, you must make decisions on how to balance everyone's needs. You likely do not want to push away people you value as friends, but you also do not want to upset them with details that present problems for them. Particularly with more emotional friends that are easily upset, you may find yourself better off avoiding situations that involve high tensions or emotions. You may turn to that friend for entertainment or for a good time, but not for highly sensitive conversations. This is not the same as walking on eggshells around the narcissist; you are still able to have a genuine relationship with these more emotionally sensitive friends, but you are also mindful of their needs as well. They may need to not hear about your difficulties for a variety of reasons, including that they may feel upset or emotionally triggered at the discussion, and as a good friend, mindful of what your friend needs, you oblige.

You also may limit situations in which these more sensitive friends have to interact with the narcissist. They may be more inclined to snapping at the narcissist than you would like, or they may feel intense negative emotions if they have escaped a relationship with a narcissist before. You can specifically look to spend time with your sensitive friends in calmer, more neutral settings, and turn to your more levelheaded friends when you need a shoulder to cry on or someone to vent to. This keeps tensions from getting too high, and you avoid setting both your friend and the narcissist up for failure. Especially when you know that your friends and the narcissist being in the same area would cause problems, it is better for everyone involved to keep them separate.

If your friends are wholly unsupportive of your choices, you may have to reevaluate your friendships, just as you reevaluate your relationships with family members. Ultimately, you need to make sure that your inner circles are supportive of you and your choices. You do not need the added stress of worrying about letting your friends or family down by making the choices you feel are the right ones.

Council from Friends

Most people go to their friends to vent their frustrations, and many friends also return those rants with suggestions on how to better the situation. Oftentimes, these suggestions are based on the other people's own life experiences. However, oftentimes, these experiences are based on normal interactions with people who are not narcissists. These suggestions oftentimes also may be counterproductive to your goal of maintaining a relationship with a narcissist. Many of your friends may tell you to break up with him or end the relationship because the behaviors are unacceptable. They also may offer suggestions to you that will only irritate or trigger the narcissist into his maladaptive behaviors, which will escalate the situation, and potentially escalate any abuse.

You will have to find a balance between trusting your friends' opinions and your desires. If your friends are demanding you cut off the narcissist and your desire is to maintain, or even further, a relationship with a narcissist, you will need to take their advice and suggestions with a grain of salt. Ultimately, your choices must work for you, with everyone else as an afterthought, so you should not feel obligated to bend to their whims just to appease them. This will take plenty of self-reflection and attempting to identify your values, as well as your goals in your relationships.

When figuring out your priorities, you will have to ask yourself what the most important thing you want is. If the most important thing is maintaining a relationship with the narcissist, then that should tip the scales in his favor when considering who to side with. Especially in cases where you are already married and have children, you may want to focus on preserving and bettering your relationship with the narcissist instead of heeding your friends' warnings of ending it before it gets worse.

On the other end of the spectrum, some of your friends' advice could be downright dangerous. If the narcissist is known to be particularly aggressive when provoked, confronting him and telling him you refuse to take this behavior, as advised by your friend, may just be adding fuel to the fire. Along with weighing your own goals, you need to maintain your own safety, and sometimes, your friends' advice would do more harm than good. What will work in ordinary relationships will not work with narcissists, and your friends might not know this.

CHAPTER 12

Kids Involved

When children are involved, navigating the waters of a narcissistic relationship become infinitely rougher. A relationship with a narcissist already involves a major juggling act as you try to balance challenging his maladaptive schemas through your own behavior, keeping from triggering him into acting on his schemas, and making sure your own needs are met, and as soon as children come into the picture, all of the pins you have been so precariously juggling are suddenly on fire. Everything has to be far more precise, and you have to take special care to not drop the pins, but also to avoid burning yourself or those you love.

You may worry that your child's own self-esteem will be damaged by the narcissist's fragile ego if the narcissist lashes out, or that your child will be on the receiving end of manipulative tactics. You also may worry that your child will learn the narcissist's behaviors through exposure and try to emulate them, or will internalize that that is the normal way to treat people within the relationship you share with the narcissist. They may think that manipulation is normal in a romantic relationship, or that it is normal to seek attention and admiration when they are a parent or grandparent if the narcissist is your mother or father. All of these are legitimate, valid fears, and unfortunately, those are very real possibilities.

Despite these possibilities, there are ways to mitigate damage while you maintain your relationship with the narcissist, or if they are forced to maintain a relationship with the narcissist due to a court order in the event of custody or grandparent rights dictating that the narcissist is to have some degree of visitation. You will have to work hard with your children to explain what narcissism is and foster the skills your children will need to become healthy, productive adults without maladaptive schemas.

You also have to know that sometimes, cutting off the relationship is in the best interest of your children in order to minimize contact with the narcissist in the event that your children are being impacted so negatively that you cannot assuage the damage. When trying to help children navigate the madhouse that is narcissism, there are three key points to remember.

Articulation is Key

Ultimately, the most important thing for children navigating narcissism is giving them an age-appropriate understanding of what is happening. Knowledge is power, and the more the children understand, the more able they will be to avoid falling into the narcissist's traps. Even if you have chosen to split apart from the narcissist, having an age-appropriate conversation about why you have made that decision will help the child. Honesty is the best policy when dealing with children, and the sooner they learn why certain people behave the way they do, the sooner they will be able to deal with it their own way.

Imagine your child has a narcissistic father. He has the tendency to be harshly critical of the child if he feels his child is not behaving the way he expects.

Even the smallest of missteps are treated like grievous mistakes, and he has a tendency to say, "You never do anything right," every time it happens. Even spilling a few drops of milk is regarded as disastrous to the narcissist. Explaining to your child that daddy has a hard time when things go wrong, and that is why he reacts that way may help your child understand. This helps your child to develop empathy and compassion for the narcissist without affirming that the narcissist's behaviors are acceptable. Remind your child that he or she is safe with you and that daddy just needs a few minutes to calm down and deal with his big feelings, just as you would likely tell your own child if she were in need of a few minutes to compose herself.

Older children may be prepared to have more in-depth conversations about what a personality disorder is and what that entails. Explaining to your children that the narcissist cannot see things around him for what they really are may aid them in learning that the narcissist's sharp words should not be given much of an afterthought. Teach them that it is not much different than a younger child calling them a meanie-head or saying that the child hates them. In a sense, this is true- the narcissist never developed relationship skills past a child's level, and therefore, a lot of his behavior is quite childish and selfish.

When having a conversation about cutting off another person, it is important to discuss with the child that sometimes, people are not safe people and it is better to stay away from them than it is to try to continue a relationship. Explain to the child that it is your job as the parent to keep them safe, and if it comes down to it, taking the children away from that person, even if it is a beloved relative, is better for everyone. Tell your children that even though they love candy, your job as a parent is to not let them have so much candy that they get sick, develop health issues, or rot their teeth. Likewise, it is your job to keep them away from people who are not safe or who make bad choices.

No matter what your end goal is with your relationship with the narcissist, remember that keeping your children informed with age-appropriate information is a key step to keeping them from being physically or emotionally harmed. Children are far smarter than most adults give them credit for, and they see more than most people expect. They will see your struggles with a narcissist, and it is better to explain it than for them to think that is just a normal interaction in a relationship. They will take your words at face value most of the time, so explain it as thoroughly as you think is appropriate. Most importantly, answer any questions they may have honestly in an age-appropriate manner. Remember that your articulation will set the stage for what your children are absorbing.

No Apologies

While you should explain the narcissist's behaviors to your children, you should never offer apologies for the narcissist. Offering apologies that the narcissist has not expressed only makes the child think that things will be different in the future, and sets up expectations that will likely not be met. Apologies imply feeling bad or recognizing the behavior is wrong, but the narcissist does not feel bad for his behaviors and does not see them as wrong.

Rather than apologizing for negative behaviors, you should instead take the option of explaining the reasoning for them. Do not think of this as excusing the behavior, or telling your children that it is acceptable to act any way they please so long as they can explain it away. This instead allows your child to begin to understand the narcissist's perspective, which is yet another exercise in empathy. The child begins to see the narcissist's side of things without learning to do the behaviors because the child learns it is essentially an illness that is causing it.

By treating the behaviors as a symptom of a mental health issue and emphasizing that keeping themselves mentally healthy is important, you teach your children to have compassion. Just as they would not judge someone in their class who is in a wheelchair and needs extra accommodations, they learn not to judge the narcissist for needing extra emotional support. They will be able to recognize his behaviors as symptoms of a problem that needs treatment rather than the narcissist being truly evil.

Perhaps your children have a narcissistic grandfather. He has a tendency to favor one and treat the other as an afterthought, and because of this, you have chosen to limit contact between your children and their grandfather. Rather than apologizing to your child who has been scapegoated, you should explain the behavior. You can tell your child that grandpa does not understand how his treatment makes her feel bad. Justify your daughter's feelings and let her know it is right to feel wronged and that it is not okay to hurt other people. You can further explain that because grandpa does not understand that hurting other people's feelings is why you are taking some time away from him.

During this explanation, do not make your children feel like they are in the wrong for feeling how they do. They will get plenty of gaslighting or thinking that they are wrong about how they understand the world around them, from the narcissist without you defending the narcissist's behaviors. Ultimately, your children need honesty at an age-appropriate level and general explanations of why the narcissist behaves how he does. They will eventually come to learn that the narcissist's behaviors are the opposite of what they want to do if you are thorough about your explanations and emulate and guide your children through learning to act with empathy and compassion.

Freedom to Express

The best thing you can do for your children that are exposed to narcissism is to foster empathy in them. By teaching your children empathy, you will foster an understanding of what behaviors are reasonable, and why some people sometimes react inappropriately. In seeing you try to work with the narcissist and help the narcissist learn adaptive behavior, your children will see that you value your relationships and will try to do what you can to understand and work around problems. They will see your caring, nurturing side that made you attractive to the narcissist in the first place, and they will learn to try their hardest to salvage a relationship before abandoning it when it is safe to do so.

Likewise, they will see what an inappropriate reaction to stress looks like, and you will teach them to have the compassion to help guide the stressed person through their inappropriate reaction. This conversation about inappropriate reactions also opens the door to explaining healthier coping mechanisms to your children. Guiding them through how to properly deal with stress in a way that will not have negative impacts on other people and will allow them to cope in a healthy manner is a life skill all people need. These conversations become learning opportunities that begin even more conversations, especially when the narcissist's behaviors can be so confusing to children. So long as you are honest about your explanations and objective about what you consider proper or improper reactions, your children will follow your lead, and if they are at an age where they are choosing their own actions, you will give them the knowledge and skills they will need to make informed choices about the narcissist on their own.

By validating your children's feelings when they discuss the narcissist, you are letting them know that they are entitled to how they feel, no matter how it is. Your empathy and compassion for your children will teach them that they can come to you if they need to, and give them the proof they need to be less vulnerable to the narcissist's behaviors. Even though you will be there, it is inevitable that they will not be exposed to some of the narcissist's maladaptive behaviors at some point, and it is best for your children to be well-prepared when that day comes.

Dealing with a Narcissist

SECTION 4

Bonus Chapters

CHAPTER 13

Helpful Mobile Apps to Make Dealing with a Narcissist Bearable

Communication with a narcissist can be especially difficult if you have ended your relationship with him or her but are required to maintain contact. Most often, the reason for required contact is when you share children. Communicating can become messy if the narcissist decides to direct his attention or rage at you. You may find him calling all hours of the night, asking inane things for the umpteenth time, like what time does

Johnny have to be at soccer, or when is Kate's parent-teacher conference. He may call you incessantly to get information or switch to messaging you on social media or via texts. This can make it difficult to track all communication, as it is constantly changing from form to form, and in many states, you cannot record another person without his or her consent. Luckily, there are a handful of apps that can be used to record and document everything from shared calendars, messages, child support, and anything else you and your narcissistic co-parent would ever need to communicate about with one another.

OurFamilyWizard

The most commonly recommended app is OurFamilyWizard[3]. This app is comprehensive and is frequently ordered in court orders for families where abuse, either verbal or physical, has occurred. Communication with this app is court-approved, and according to their website, is recommended by courts in all 50 states of America to be used to manage co-parenting communication. This app allows for calendars to be shared, expenses to be tracked, files shared, and allows for the parents to share messages back and forth with one another.

This site also includes access for professionals to communicate with both parents. Doctors, lawyers, counselors, mediators, and other professionals will be able to communicate and view communication between the parents, so there is no denying what the narcissist said. Everything is documented in black and white for professionals involved in your custody case to see.

One unique feature of OurFamilyWizard includes is its ToneMeter. This is essentially a grammar checker, but it gauges tone instead of grammar. This flags when a sentence written has been emotionally charged, allowing the writer to see the tone of what is being written so it can be corrected and written in a way that may be more productive or better received. Since oftentimes, the tone is lost in translation with written correspondence, this can help both you and the narcissist word things in a way that are less inflammatory.

Overall, this app is great if you are in a high conflict shared parenting relationship. This will allow you to limit in-person or verbal communication, and will also allow for easier documentation.

Coparently

Coparently[4] is quite similar to OurFamilyWizard. It allows for parents to digitally share information pertaining to their children quickly in one place for easy tracking and documenting. This app keeps everything you could possibly need together and allows you and your co-parent to share calendars, messages to each other, manage expenses, and a list of contacts that are relevant to your children, such as their doctors, schools, extracurricular activities, daycares, or friends' parents. All of that communication and information in one place means you have to contact your ex significantly less, and when you do contact one another, it is all in one place and easily tracked and documented.

This app works on virtually any electronic device, with versions available for Android, iPhone, BlackBerry, Windows Phones, and Kindle Fire Devices. There are also desktop versions for all major operating systems and modern browsers. With such a wide range of ways to contact one another, you never have to worry about cross-compatibility again. You can also give guest access to your account, allowing professionals to see and monitor communication methods. There is also a special children's

Helpful Mobile Apps to Make Dealing with a Narcissist Bearable

mode that allows kids to see the calendars, keeping them informed on what will be happening with them when.

This allows for all of the communication that is necessary to be passed back and forth for co-parenting effectively, while still maintaining some semblance of distance. Since all communication can be monitored, the narcissist will likely be on his best behavior to avoid being painted as the bad guy in the divorce. Pricing is available on their website, and at the time of writing this book, they were offering a free 30-day trial to decide if it is right for you.

2houses

2houses[5] is yet another mobile app that seeks to consolidate all of the information coparents need to be successful. This app is compatible with Android, iOS, and internet browsers, and offers a 14-day free trial at the time of this book's writing. They include access to a messenger, calendar, financial tracker, an info-bank where you can store all of your children's pertinent information, photo albums that allow for photos and memories to be shared, and a journal where you can record funny, cute, or interesting information about what has happened on your custody time to document your child's growth.

This site allows parents to grant access to other users as well and can specify how much or how little the others are able to see. This app also allows for you to set up multiple profiles under the same email address so if you require more than one family account, you are able to have them all created for the same email address.

Ultimately, this is yet another app meant to share information between co-parents without having actual physical or verbal contact with one another. The added features of being able to easily document a journal and share media files with one another is a welcome addition. With the added areas of contact with this form of communication such as the journal, it may be best to be used with exes lower on the narcissistic spectrum that would not be seeking to wreak as much havoc on your life as others.

Overcome Narcissism Self & Ego by Angie Atkinson

This app is different in that it is about overcoming narcissism instead of creating ways to communicate that mitigate abuse. Overcome Narcissism Self & Ego by Angie Atkinson[6] includes audio content about surviving narcissistic abuse, techniques to alleviate anxiety, and meditations and affirmations created by Angie Atkinson, a life coach. She regularly adds new content to the site on a multitude of topics that will help you navigate through healing from narcissistic abuse.

With this free mobile app, you will have access to certain content right from downloading, and you can purchase more. The content will give you ways to identify narcissistic behavior, resources for recovering, basic guides to what to expect, and more. If you feel lost and unsure where to go from here in your journey to healing or you would like some more content to listen to daily, this app will be beneficial to you.

CHAPTER 14

25 Helpful Affirmations for Dealing with a Narcissist

Affirmations are fantastic tools to keep yourself level-headed. Often used paired with mindfulness or during various therapies, affirmations are short, simple phrases for you to repeat to yourself during times of stress to ground yourself and keep from letting your emotions or bad habits get the best of you. Affirmations can be anything, though they have three basic rules. The first rule is that they must be about yourself. This is because you are only able to control yourself. You cannot dictate how other people perceive or interact with the world, but you can control your own thoughts or actions. The second rule is that it must be positive. By focusing on positive language, you put yourself into a positive mindset. Think of the difference between, "I will not fall into my old habits," versus "I am taking steps to change my behavior to get the results I want." Between the two, the second is more inspiring. The third rule is that the affirmation must be worded in a way that is in the present tense. This way, you remind yourself that it is true at that particular moment because that is what you are experiencing. With these three rules, you can create any sort of affirmations you think will be useful to you and your situation.

Affirmations can come in many different forms, and having an arsenal of affirmations about a broad range of struggles can help you in almost any situation. Do you have a hard time trusting yourself? Repeat some mental clarity affirmations. Are you struggling to do what you need for yourself? Remind yourself of your self-worth with affirmations. This chapter will provide you with affirmations for clarity, compassion, patience, self-worth, and healing to help you on your journey. Remember to repeat these to yourself as you need them, and you will be able to keep yourself grounded, even in times of high emotion.

Affirmations of Mental Clarity

My perceptions of reality are accurate, and I will trust them to guide me through making decisions.

Narcissists are masters at manipulating others. They love to gaslight, convincing you that what you believe happened did not occur the way you think, or that it did not happen at all. Narcissists have a tendency to say things to get you to doubt yourself and believe their side of the story. This could be especially unsettling if you were already struggling with trusting yourself before, as you now have someone you likely respect a great deal telling you that you are wrong about what you think happened. You begin to feel like you are going crazy. This is what the narcissist wants, as it makes you easier to control. By repeating this affirmation to yourself, you are able to remind yourself that your own judgments are worthy of trust. Any time you are feeling doubtful about how you perceive something, you can remind yourself that you are trustworthy and your perceptions are accurate. Trust your judgment and follow your gut reactions, even if the narcissist tries to convince you to do otherwise.

25 Helpful Affirmations for Dealing with a Narcissist

I have the experience to see through attempts to manipulate me, and the strength to make sure I can stand firm against them. I have withstood the storm once, and I will do it this time as well.

This affirmation reminds you to use your experiences of being manipulated in the past to key into whether you are being manipulated in the present. If you are interacting with the narcissist in your life and begin to doubt yourself, reminding yourself that you can see through the manipulation. You also remind yourself that you were strong enough to get through the manipulation in the past, and you are even stronger now that you are standing up to it. Your strength will help you avoid being manipulated in the future.

I am grateful that I can see things for what they are, and that I know I can trust my judgment.

Reminding yourself that you are grateful for your clarity reminds you to never take that clarity for granted- it was earned through hard work and struggles. Your mental clarity came through adversity, and you have learned to see through the manipulative tactics that the narcissist employs through the first-hand experience. Reminding yourself that you are grateful for your clarity reminds you once again that it is valuable and trustworthy. When you begin to doubt yourself, reminding that you value your perceptions reminds you to rely on them rather than believing anyone who convinces you to doubt them.

I can clearly see my goals for this relationship in my mind, and I am actively taking steps toward that goal.

Reminding yourself that you know exactly what you hope to achieve reminds yourself that you know what you need best. If someone tries to make you doubt you know what is best, or tries to convince you to do something you are unsure of or disagree with, you can remind yourself that your own clarity is ultimately what you need to rely on, not what other people think you need or want. You also remind yourself that you are working on your goals any time you feel doubtful you are on track or like you are doing the wrong things for the wrong reasons.

My mental clarity brings me the strength I need to overcome any challenges or obstacles that get in the way of completing my goals and the wisdom to know when it is time to change my goas.

This affirmation reminds you that your clarity is your strength. Knowing you can trust yourself to see the world around you clearly will enable you to get past any manipulative or degrading behavior the narcissist may subject you to. Your goals are clear in your mind and you know exactly what you want. Your clarity also lets you see things for what they are so you can recognize when your goals are no longer viable, so you do not find yourself stuck in a sunk cost fallacy, believing that you have to keep going toward something that does not make sense because you have already put in a lot of energy toward it. Sometimes, knowing when to quit is important and practical.

Affirmations of Compassion

I have the compassion, patience and grace to get through this difficult time.

Reminding yourself that you have compassion and patience can be the difference between snapping and saying something in anger. That moment to take a deep breath and recite your affirmation will help if you ever feel like you are losing your patience. We all have moments when our patience is tested, and we have to remind ourselves to stay calm and collected. When the narcissist begins pushing your buttons, what he is seeking is a reaction to affirm a maladaptive schema. You reacting in anger would likely reaffirm the schema, so reminding yourself of your immense compassion and patience will keep you calm enough to avoid reactive behavior.

Any mistakes I or others make are simple missteps and they deserve to be treated with compassion and understanding.

Sometimes it can be hard to remain calm and react in a productive manner when someone messes up, even if the mistake is harmless. It is still an inconvenience to fix the mistake, no matter how small. Oftentimes, people are compassionate with other people who make mistakes and understand how it could have happened, but they are harsh on themselves. You are just as deserving as compassion after making a mistake as anyone else. After all, you are only human, and humans are not perfect. Making mistakes is a normal part of life, and by treating yourself kindly through the mistakes, no matter how big or small, you will help yourself become stronger and learn from what happened. This also reminds you to be gentle with the narcissist when he or she does something that is unkind or unexpected. Your understanding of narcissistic personality disorder will help you remain compassionate and firm in your goals of either maintaining a relationship or ending one.

I recognize that my compassion lets me see the best in others and gives me insight to be my best self.

When you realize that, despite the fact that the narcissist used it to his advantage, your compassion is a strength, you begin to embrace it. Being able to see the best in others is a blessing; you can see potential where work in progress is standing, and you can provide those around you with the support they will need in order to become that potential. This will also allow you to see the best in the narcissist, which may be buried under scars and maladaptive behavior, but you will be able to acknowledge the parts of the narcissist that you truly enjoy and embrace. These will be your reminders of why you want to maintain your relationship, as you see the narcissist beyond his flaws.

My respect and compassion for others reflect on my true character.

Remember, you cannot control how other people use your help, but not helping at all out of fear that your aid would be misused would ultimately reflect your character. Your compassionate nature is who you are, and recognizing that compassion as who you are can remind you to remain compassionate, even when it is the harder choice.

Sometimes, it is harder to maintain contact with someone than it is to walk away, but maintaining that contact is the right choice. When maintaining contact with the narcissist, although difficult, is right for you even though walking away would be easier, reminding yourself that you are the kind of person that stays and aids others, even when it is tough, will keep your resolve strong.

I choose to treat everyone with compassion and respect because treating them with respect makes my world a more compassionate place.

Ultimately, you cannot control other people. Even the narcissist, the master manipulator, cannot fully control those around him. What you can control, however, is you. By treating others with compassion, you make your world a slightly more compassionate place. Your compassion creates a ripple effect that will hopefully do some good outside of your initial actions. Perhaps it inspires someone else to do a good deed. Maybe it helps the narcissist challenge one of his maladaptive schemas. Either way, your compassion is never wasted, even on someone who misuses the grace you give, because you are being true to yourself, even when you know it might be wasted.

25 Helpful Affirmations for Dealing with a Narcissist

Affirmations of Self-worth

My empathy and compassion are my greatest strengths, and despite the narcissist taking advantage of them, I am proud to be myself.

This affirmation reasserts that your empathy and compassion are strengths and not weaknesses, even though they were what the narcissist used to get what was wanted from you in the first place. The vast majority of the world sees your convictions and sees a wonderful, kindhearted person who is understanding and caring. You should always remember that you are valuable, and your strengths define who you are. That strength will take you far in life, and you should be proud to be you, even when you are beginning to doubt yourself.

Humans deserve to be treated with basic care and respect, and I deserve this too.

Narcissists often degrade your sense of duty to yourself. You spend so long worrying about the narcissist and catering to the narcissist's needs that you forget that you deserve it as well. After so long of being discarded as an afterthought, even you may begin to regard yourself as one. Reminding yourself that you are just as deserving as everyone else of basic care and respect will keep you taking care of yourself as well. After all, no one is ever as invested in caring for you than yourself! You would not let your phone or laptop battery die if it can be helped, and you should treat your own emotional battery the same. Recharge when you need it, even if you do not feel as if you deserve it, because you do deserve it, just like everyone else deserves to recharge.

I am deserving of love, kindness, and compassion, just like everyone else in the world.

The narcissist may have repeatedly told you that no one could ever love you as you are, or that everyone is only using you. The irony here is that he was only deflecting his own feelings onto you. He feels as if he is unlovable, so he lashes out at others. Just as you feel compassionate and kind toward others, you need to reflect some of that kindness toward yourself as well. Loving yourself is one of the first steps toward healing and having a healthy sense of self. Even in moments where you doubt yourself and wonder if the narcissist is right, remind yourself that you, like everyone else, are worthy of love.

25 Helpful Affirmations for Dealing with a Narcissist

I deserve the kind of healthy, stable relationships I crave, and I am taking steps to make them.

Another part of loving or respecting your self is making sure the relationships you surround yourself with are healthy. You deserve healthy relationships; no one deserves abuse or torment, and especially not from the person they have chosen to devote themselves to. Reminding yourself that you are taking steps toward healthy relationships can help you avoid situations that may become toxic, and recognize that sometimes, the only right answer is to leave a relationship to protect yourself, and you deserve to do that for yourself if it is the only solution.

I am worthy of loving myself and recognizing my strengths and the value I bring to other people.

This affirmation reminds you to never devalue yourself. Narcissists oftentimes purposefully put you down and tell you that you are worth less than you actually are. They want you to feel worthless so you feel trapped. By reminding yourself of how valuable you actually are to those you love and who love you, you remind yourself to treat yourself better. You have already spent time being belittled and demeaned, and there is no reason for you to perpetuate the narcissist's abuse to yourself.

Affirmations of Patience

I have the patience to get through these tests and the mental clarity to understand that I cannot control others.

Reminding yourself that you are patient enough to handle difficult situations helps you remain calm during even the most testing situations. Keep in mind that oftentimes, when dealing with a narcissist, he wants you to react negatively as that reaffirms everything he believes is true. By also acknowledging that you cannot control the narcissist, no matter how much easier that would make life, you remind yourself to keep your patience when things do not go as you were hoping them to. The narcissist will rarely react the way you would expect or hope, so recognizing that you cannot control him is a big step toward maintaining your composure.

I am flexible and I can roll with anything life throws at me with patience and perseverance.

Along with the previous affirmation, acknowledging that you cannot control the world around you, but you can control your own reaction will give you a sense of control over the situation. Knowing you can control your reactions and reminding yourself of this will help you to consciously make decisions that you are sure will be beneficial and productive as opposed to acting in inflammatory ways that only make the situation worse.

I have plenty of patience to care for myself and those I love.

Sometimes, the narcissist or other people we love are draining on our patience and good will. We feel as if our patience is a finite resource, and it is quickly running empty. This affirmation reminds you that you do have the patience you need, and that you are enough for yourself and others. Sometimes, what you need is a little reminder that you do have enough patience for everyone to be able to get through whatever trying event is happening.

My patience and my understanding nature will guide me through even the toughest times with those I love.

When things are going rough, it can be hard to remember that you need to remain calm. Especially when someone you love is doing something that hurts you or makes you unhappy, you may find yourself reacting rather than acting calmly. The narcissist will test and push you, looking for ways to prove he is right and you are reactionary. You need to remind yourself that your patience will help you remain calm, even when things get bad.

I stay calm even under stress.

Sometimes, the simplest affirmations are the most helpful in stressful situations. When you are beginning to feel overwhelmed, take a deep breath and repeat this affirmation to yourself before exhaling. After a couple of repetitions, you should be in a calmer mindset and able to take on whatever is stressing you at that moment.

Affirmations of Healing

I am healing, and every day, I get a little bit closer to finishing that process.

Healing is a difficult process, even in the best of situations. We often take one step forward and feel like we immediately fall back two steps as well. The grief and pain often feel like it ebbs and flows, and on the days when the pain is overwhelming, you may feel like you are failing. Remember, the pain means you are healing, and every day, you get one step closer to the wounds inflicted by the narcissist healing. Even when you feel like you are failing and the pain is worse, you are still moving closer to becoming whole once more. Take a moment to remind yourself of this when you feel at your lowest.

I am taking care of myself to promote healing and good health.

Sometimes, the effort of caring for yourself can feel impossible after the devastating effects of the narcissist on your life. The narcissist's influence over you can feel so overwhelming that you feel as though caring for yourself is undeserved and unnecessary. Remind yourself that the effort you are exerting to care for yourself is absolutely necessary when you are healing. Just as you would protect a broken leg and avoid bearing weight while it heals, you should care for yourself as well. You need extra attention and care during that time.

I am leaving my past behind me in order to make the future what I want it to be.

Oftentimes, we have a tendency to focus on the past. We get preoccupied with our struggles, and the pain from the past follows us, making it feel like it is happening in present time all over again. Reminding yourself that the past is over and cannot be changed can help you turn your focus from ruminating to working toward bettering yourself for the future to avoid that pain. While it is unhealthy to dwell on the past, it is healthy to learn from it so you can do better in the future. That reminder is sometimes necessary, especially on days when you find yourself missing the early stages of your relationship with the narcissist.

I know my future will be worth any troubles I am facing now, and I am keeping my mind focused on my goals.

Sometimes, when things get hard, we think it might be easier to go back to the way things used to be. At the very least, that pain is familiar, while the healing process may be entirely foreign to you. You may be missing the narcissist, or feeling lonely and worthless. No matter what the reason, reminding yourself that the troubles are temporary and are a necessary evil to get to the future that you desire will help keep you on track. You can use this to remind yourself to not give in to temptation of returning your old way of life. Remember, even though it is familiar, that life was not easy, or you would not have been seeking to change it in the first place.

It is my duty to protect myself and I owe it to myself to make sure I am taken care of and safe, even if I have to do things that are difficult to ensure it.

Ultimately, you are responsible for yourself. You owe it to yourself to take care of yourself, even if doing so is difficult or requires you to make sacrifices. If the only way to feel like you are healthy or whole is to give up on a relationship that brings you pain, no matter how hard it is, you owe it to yourself to do it. You must not sacrifice yourself for others, especially if they will not appreciate the effort or will only hurt you in return. If the narcissist is toxic, you have no business remaining in that relationship.

Thank you for reading my book...

Don't forget to leave an honest review...

I'd like to offer you this amazing resource which my clients pay for. It is a report I written when I first began my journey.

Click on the picture above or navigate to the website below to join my exclusive email list. Upon joining, you will receive this incredible report on how to recognize an abusive relationship.

If you ask most people on the street what an abusive relationship is, chances are you'd get a description of physical abuse. And yes, that is most certainly an abusive relationship. However, abuse comes in many forms. The actual meaning of abuse is when someone exerts control over another person.

Find out more about recognizing an abusive relationship and learn how to take control over your life by clicking on the book above or by going to this link:

http://bit.ly/RecognizeAbusiveRelationship

Dealing with a Narcissist

CONCLUSION

Congratulations! You have made it to the end of the book. One of the hardest steps is acknowledging that you have a problem that needs to be fixed, and in seeking out this book, you likely have, at least to some degree. You may be suspecting that something is wrong in one of your relationships and are exploring options. Or perhaps someone you know is a narcissist and you wanted to know whether the relationship was worth attempting to salvage. Whatever your reason for picking up this book, you have been provided with valuable information about how to navigate the world of narcissism.

Through this book, you were given insight into what narcissistic personality disorder is, as well as how to treat it through schema therapy. Understanding that narcissism is caused as reactive, maladaptive coping mechanisms against stress will help you empathize and understand why the narcissist behaves how he or she does. It also provides insight into how to interact with the narcissist, through identifying certain schemas you suspect the narcissist has developed and interacting in ways that contradict the schemas. These skills are valuable assets when you either desire to maintain a relationship with a narcissist, or you have no choice but to continue contact. You were provided with suggestions for how to interact with others around you that do not understand what a relationship with a narcissist entails, and how to weigh suggestions from the uninformed with those you care about's feelings on the matter, and your own goals. With these skills, as well as some helpful apps and affirmations, you are a little more prepared to hold your own with a narcissist than you were before.

Ultimately, this is a long, arduous journey. Even cutting the narcissist off does not end the journey, as you will still have a long road to trek as you heal. However, you can do this. As difficult as it may be, you can learn to interact with a narcissist and you can mitigate damage and how

Conclusion

often you fall for the narcissist's tactics. Trust yourself on this journey and follow your own pace. Regardless of whether you choose to maintain a relationship beyond a superficial level or if you desire to cut off the narcissist for good, find a support group. Do not be afraid to reach out to others who understand what you are going through. That support is essential to you, and you may find it is a valuable resource you never knew you needed.

Keep moving forward and keep your head up! Even if you feel hopeless or as if you cannot get through this, remember, that you can, and you will. Even setbacks, small or large, do not mean you are destined for failure, and you do not have to live your life unhappily. Choose what you truly want as your goal, and work toward it. Think of things one day, one hour, or one minute at a time if that is all you can get through at the moment, and keep putting your feet one step in front of the other. You will make it to the other side if you keep moving toward it.

References, Resources, and Helpful Links

1. Edelstein, R. S., Yim, I. S., & Quas, J. A. (2010, June 25). Narcissism predicts heightened cortisol reactivity to a psychosocial stressor in men. Retrieved from https://www.sciencedirect.com/science/article/abs/pii/S0092656610000917

2. What is Schema-Focused Therapy? (2017, August 23). Retrieved from https://www.pasadenavilla.com/2017/04/05/what-is-schema-focused-therapy/

3. OurFamilyWizard. Retrieved from https://www.ourfamilywizard.com/

4. Coparently. Retrieved from http://coparently.com/

5. 2houses. Retrieved from https://www.2houses.com/en/

6. Atkinson, A. Overcome Narcissism Self & Ego by Angie Atkinson - Apps on Google Play. Retrieved from https://play.google.com/store/apps/details?id=com.pitashi.audiojoy.angieatkinson&hl=en_US

www.ingramcontent.com/pod-product-compliance
Lightning Source LLC
Chambersburg PA
CBHW020255030426
42336CB00010B/777